POPULAR SOVEREIGNTY
AND THE
FRENCH CONSTITUENT ASSEMBLY
1789–91

POPULAR SOVEREIGNTY AND THE FRENCH CONSTITUENT ASSEMBLY
1789-91

by

ERIC THOMPSON

M.A.(Com.), B.Sc.(Econ.), Ph.D.

MANCHESTER UNIVERSITY PRESS

Published by the University of Manchester at
THE UNIVERSITY PRESS
316–324, Oxford Road, Manchester 13
1952

Printed in Great Britain by Butler & Tanner Ltd., Frome and London

CONTENTS

PREFACE

TOWARDS the end of the eighteenth century in France, the concept of the sovereignty of the 'general will' of the people had been widely disseminated amongst the mass of the people. It is true that the more elaborate treatment of the nature of the sovereign power, which had been contained in the works of Rousseau and other major treatises published during the second half of the century, was probably little known outside a small circle of intellectuals. But the concept of popular sovereignty itself had been popularised in thousands of pamphlets, which had served up to the wider public garbled and inaccurate versions of the greater works and, often in flamboyant language, had helped to spread a myth, and develop a *mystique*, that each citizen, by virtue of his 'natural rights', was, in very fact, a participant in the sovereign power in the State.

As Augustin Cochin has pointed out, the growth of this *mystique* had also been fostered by the *sociétés de pensée* and the masonic lodges which had been established in large numbers throughout the country. And, as he emphasises, there was no obscurity or vagueness in the popular mind about this *mystique*. 'Nothing could be clearer or more lucid', he writes, 'than the idealism of the eighteenth century.'

Thus, when the deputies of the Third Estate met at Versailles in 1789, they had behind them a considerable volume of popular support, couched in terms of a popular idealism, which was based upon this concept of the sovereignty of the 'general will'. On July 14th of that year the 'people' were to demonstrate the strength of this particular *mystique*; they were to insist that both King and aristocracy should realise where lay the sovereign power in the State.

In this work, which in its original form was submitted for the Doctorate in Philosophy of the University of London, an attempt is made to trace the influence of the concept on the constitutional ideas of the National Assembly, and the way in which it was modified to meet the various difficulties encountered by the deputies in drawing up a Constitution for their country. In effect, a notable evolution of the concept took place, not only as a result of efforts to adapt a somewhat nebulous idea to the harsh realities of the constitution-making process, but because of its employment as a first line of defence against subversive tendencies in the State, whether these originated from the Right or from the extreme Left. As finally embodied in the Constitution of 1791, the doctrine of the sovereignty of the 'general will' of the people was, in the event, to bear but little resemblance to that concept which was so popular in 1789, and which had been embodied in the famous Declaration of the Rights of Man and of the Citizen of that year.

The author is deeply indebted to the late Professor Harold J. Laski and to Dr. C. A. Cooke, of Magdalen College, Oxford, for much helpful advice and criticism. Neither of these gentlemen has, of course, any responsibility for the opinions expressed, or conclusions reached, in this book.

February, 1951.

INTRODUCTION

THE ESTATES GENERAL AND
THE DEADLOCK

ON May 5th, 1789, the Estates General met at Versailles after a lapse of one hundred and seventy-five years. Two hundred and eighty-five nobles, three hundred and eighty clergy and six hundred and eighty-eight members of the Third Estate had been elected. The Commons were made up of four clergy (including the Abbé Sieyès), fifteen nobles (including Mirabeau), twenty royal officials, two hundred and four municipal officers, one hundred and thirty merchants, bankers and men of independent means, fifteen doctors, one hundred and fifty men who held posts in the judicial and administrative services of the country, two hundred and ten barristers, notaries and other legal officials, and but forty peasant farmers. The Third Estate had been elected by what amounted to universal suffrage, all men of twenty-five years or more, whose names appeared on the tax registers of the country, having the right to vote. Of the Clergy, some two-thirds were *curés*, whose sympathies lay rather with the Third Estate than with their own Order.

It was thus clear that any insistence by the Commons upon a unicameral assembly, with the *vote par tête*, would reduce the two privileged Orders to a minority party in the Government. It was, therefore, over this question that a deadlock arose.

No sooner had the inaugural speeches been made than the Nobles and Clergy retired to their own chambers to verify their powers and constitute themselves, leaving the Commons in possession of a hall, the *Salle des Menus Plaisirs*, which had been intended only for joint meetings of the three Orders. For some reason Necker had omitted to provide the Commons with a separate meeting-place, an oversight which he was subsequently to regret. Nevertheless, this oversight told in his favour. The Commons assumed that in view of his insistence upon the doubling of the representation of the Third Estate, and the general tone of his Report of December 27th,[1] he had, at the

---

[1] *Résultat du Conseil* (Necker's Report), which contained the royal assent to the doubling of the representation of the Third Estate.

last moment, fallen victim to the machinations of the Court. No definite ruling had, however, been given upon the question of a unicameral assembly. Necker had not specifically referred to the matter. The King withdrew from the inaugural ceremonies without giving a decision.

Left to themselves, the Third Estate had to decide upon a course of action. The fate of the Revolution was in the balance. Were they to follow the procedure of the Clergy and Nobility and to verify their powers as a separate Order? Such a course would deprive them of all the advantages of double representation, for it would give the privileged Orders a right of veto upon all decisions they might reach.

The Commons did not hesitate. Strengthened by the uncompromising attitude of the Breton deputies,[1] inspired by the leadership of Mirabeau,[2] and under the eyes of the 'sovereign people', they decided to do precisely nothing. In terms of the *mystique* which had already become current amongst the more intellectual members of the democratic party—and the deputies of the Third Estate were of this number—they based their conduct upon the principle that as the sovereign power in the State lay in the 'general will' of the nation, such a will could be ascertained only by the elected representatives of the whole of the nation, gathered together in unitary assembly. As the deputies of the Third Estate did not represent the entire nation, no such 'general will' could be ascertained until they had been joined by the deputies of the other two Orders. Hence, as they were not properly constituted, the Commons had no power to act. They could carry out no business; they could not even despatch official deputations to the Nobles and Clergy with a view to securing their adherence. Thus there commenced a period of inaction, during which the Commons, as trustees of the public purse, held the master card. 'The battle', wrote a deputy from Lorraine, 'has begun.' It was to last until June 27th.

The course of events during the ensuing period is well known. The individual contacts between the Orders which took place despite the Commons' ban on deputations; the obstinacy of the Nobility; the willingness of the Clergy to negotiate; the continuing indecision and pusillanimity of the King; the doubts which began to assail the more

---

[1] Cf. especially A. Bouchard: *Le Club Breton* (Paris, 1920), pp. 16 f.

[2] On the leadership of Mirabeau, and the great influence of his political ideas during the early days of the National Assembly, cf. Pierre Duclos: *La Notion de Constitution dans l'Œuvre de l'Assemblée Constituante de 1789* (Paris, 1932), pp. 55 f.

responsible members of the Commons as to the wisdom of their course of action—doubts which led not only Malouet and Mounier, but even Robespierre and Mirabeau to suggest means whereby the deadlock might be broken. And the steadfast refusal of the Commons to entertain any thought of compromise.

As the weeks went by, the deputies of the Third Estate became more and more impatient. Tempers became frayed, and the news that the Nobles had 'sufficiently and legally' constituted themselves, which reached the Commons on May 13th, added fuel to the flames. Their answer was delivered by Le Chapelier. 'The deputies of the Commons declare that they will recognise as legal representatives of the nation only those deputies whose powers have been examined by the commissioners appointed in the Estates General by all those summoned to compose it, as it is the concern not only of the privileged bodies, but also of the body representative of the whole nation to know of, and pass judgment upon, the validity of the powers of the deputies who present themselves, each and every deputy belonging to the General Assembly.'

Considerable unrest resulted in the Commons. 'Do they (the privileged Orders) know to what we may be forced?' demanded Reubell. 'May we not be forced to declare ourselves the nation, and to commence our work of restoring the Monarchy without the assistance of all the persons presumably legally elected by the Clergy and the Nobility as deputies to the Estates General? I claim that we may perhaps be compelled to take this course.' The Breton deputies supported this point of view.[1] But the majority of the Commons were generally against hasty action. As Boissy d'Anglas said:

'Your mandates, gentlemen, and your individual wishes are in perfect accord, and the universality of the deputies of the Third Estate, representing twenty-five million people from whom they have received their powers, believe it to be indispensable for the good of the State, the property of the nation and the affirmation of common liberty, that in the Assembly all voices should be counted by head. This question has already been determined by the unanimity of our mandates. The prayers of the people are our orders, their complaints our laws. They are essentially the nation, whereas the other Orders are but dependants of it. Nevertheless, gentlemen, the firmer and more irrevocable your attitude becomes, the more indispensable is it that it should be preceded by steps leading to conciliation and peace.'[2]

---

[1] Bouchard, op. cit., p. 65.
[2] Compare, for example, Rabaut de St. Etienne's reply to Le Chapelier: 'Destined by nature, exhorted by our Monarch himself to set sail for the land of Liberty, shall

So the deadlock continued.   On May 28th the King himself took action to bring it to an end by summoning a meeting for May 29th of all three Orders, in the presence of the Keeper of the Seals, which it was hoped would contribute to 'an instant and desirable harmony'. But, after a long reiteration of historical arguments, the meeting failed, the Nobles subsequently issuing the following statement: 'The Order of the Nobility, considering that, at this present moment, it is its bounden duty to rally to the Constitution, and give an example of firmness, as it has given proof of its disinterestedness, declares that deliberation by Order is one of those historic principles which are essential pillars of the throne and of liberty.'[1]

On June 3rd, the Commons were strengthened by the arrival of the Paris deputies.   During the following week they became increasingly anxious about the possible consequences of further inaction.   Distrust of the King was growing, as was a suspicion that the Nobles, by con-stituting themselves, might ally themselves with the King against the Commons.   Malouet again insisted upon the necessity for action, and on June 8th demanded that the Third Estate verify its powers and constitute itself as a 'Legitimate Assembly of the representatives of the Commons, acting directly with the King, and without undertaking anything against the other two Orders, and yet without recognising their veto'.[2]

There was increasing unanimity amongst the deputies that further delay was dangerous.   But such a title as that suggested by Malouet yielded too much power to the privileged Orders.   It did not emphasise the growing determination of the deputies that the sovereignty of the people should be fully recognised; it did not implement the principle of the sovereignty of the 'general will'.   Many of the more radical deputies pointed this out in forcible terms.   Ultimately, as a first step, it was decided to break the deadlock by solemnly calling the roll of deputies elected by all three Orders, and by issuing a warning to both Nobles and Clergy that deputies not presenting themselves in the *Salle des Menus Plaisirs* for this purpose would be cited as defaulters. Bailly remarked that in taking this step the Assembly 'discovered the essential principle which was the basis of the Constitution'.[3]

we leave on the beach the companions of our voyage (the First and Second Estates)? What a tragic mistake were we to allow the prestige attached to our beliefs to hold us apart from our brothers.' (*Moniteur*, 1789, p. 17.)

[1] *Journal de Versailles*, No. 1.
[2] J. S. Bailly: *Mémoires d'un Témoin de la Révolution* (Paris, 1804), Vol. I, p. 153.
[3] Ibid., p. 171.

On June 12th the roll was called, the defaulters were named, and the powers of the deputies present were verified. The immediate result was a split amongst the Clergy. Many of the lesser Clergy had already declared their sympathy for the ideas of the Third Estate. On June 13th three of them—Lecesve, Ballard and Jallet—joined the Commons. On the 14th six more, led by the Abbé Gregoire, presented themselves. Three more followed on the 15th.

The next step taken by the Commons was to adopt a title for the new Assembly. Many deputies suggested *La Nation*. Mirabeau proposed *Représentants du Peuple Français*; Mounier preferred *L'Assemblée légitime des Représentants de la majeure partie de la Nation, agissant en l'absence de la mineure partie*. Pison du Galand suggested *L'Assemblée active et légitime de la Nation française*; Barère de Vieusac liked *Représentants de la très majeure partie des Français dans l'Assemblée Nationale*. Many more titles were advocated, but ultimately, on the motion of Le Grand, the title which Sieyès had originally suggested was adopted, and the deputies incorporated themselves as the National Assembly. 'Thus', remarked Bailly, 'the Assembly compromised between tradition and reason.' It was apparent, from the rejection of the compromise titles put forward by Barère, Mounier and others, that already the more radical deputies were in a majority; that, for them, the sovereign power of the nation was to be found only in the *Salle des Menus Plaisirs*, in the hands of those deputies who most truly represented the sovereign people.

On June 17th, the National Assembly formally constituted itself. The motion was that of Sieyès:

The Assembly, deliberating after having verified its powers, recognises that it is already composed of representatives directly elected by at least ninety-six per cent of the nation. So large a deputation cannot remain inactive because of the absence of the deputies from several bailliages or several classes of citizens, for the absentees, who have been summoned, cannot prevent those present from exercising the fullness of their rights; moreover, the exercise of such rights is an imperative and a pressing duty.

Further, as the right of participation in the national government belongs only to representatives whose powers have been verified, and such representatives must be present in this Assembly, it is indispensable to conclude that the right of interpreting and determining the general will of the nation belongs to it and can belong to no other body. No veto, no power of negation can exist between the throne and the Assembly.

The Assembly therefore declares that the common task of national restoration can and must be begun without delay by the deputies present, and that it must be pursued without interruption and without admitting any obstacle.

The denomination 'National Assembly' is the only one suitable for the Assembly in the actual state of affairs, partly because its members are the only legitimate representatives whose powers have been publicly recognised and verified; partly because they have been sent by nearly the whole of the nation; partly because the representation being one and indivisible, no deputy, by whatever Order or class he may have been chosen, has the right to exercise his functions separately from this Assembly.

The Assembly will never lose hope of uniting in its bosom all the deputies absent today; it will not cease to call them to the Estates General. At whatever moment the absent deputies present themselves in the session which is about to open, it declares in advance that it will hasten to welcome them, and after verification of their powers, to share with them the great work destined to procure the regeneration of France.'

Thus the constitution of the Assembly took place. Within the limits mentioned above, the sovereignty of the people had been established, and its representatives, in co-operation with the King, were prepared not only to lay afresh the foundations of the Constitution, but to work for the alleviation of the economic and social distress which was so widespread at the time.

But the King was not equally willing to work with them. Unable to make up his mind on the issue of the *vote par tête*, he was equally unable to decide his attitude to the new Assembly. As a result, he was swayed by a reactionary Court, and the National Assembly had to confront a series of attacks which were designed to weaken its determination. Such attacks are well known. Primarily there was the closure of the *Salle des Menus Plaisirs*, which led to the historic meeting on the tennis court and the oath never to separate until the Constitution had been established; the affair of the Royal Session followed, on June 23rd, when the party of the Comte d'Artois forbade the Commons to discuss the Constitution, feudal property and the rights of the privileged Orders, and commanded them to limit their debates to the question of taxation only, each Order to continue to meet separately for this purpose. To which Mirabeau replied with his possibly too famous, 'Go tell your master that we are here by the will of the people, and nothing but bayonets shall drive us out.'

And yet the Assembly was patient with the King. The meeting on the tennis court had concluded with a vociferous *Vive le roi*. Whilst Bailly's 'constitution, perfectly wise, fundamentally just and founded on the natural rights of man' seemed a little nearer of accomplishment, it was recognised that the King must form an integral part of the legislature. A suggestion made on the tennis court, that the

Assembly should move to Paris, had been scouted because 'not the least drawback would be our separation from the King, which would lead to undesirable consequences'.[1] Later Bailly added, 'The Assembly, in its firm and courageous conduct, if it did take useful precautions against the Ministry, if it did arm itself against despotism, was yet united in heart and in spirit with the King, and had no intention of doing anything which would undermine his legitimate authority. It even took great care to declare that one of its duties was to maintain the true principles of the monarchy, in order to prove clearly that anything which may have appeared hostile in the steps which it had taken was directed specifically against despotism and not against the monarchy itself.'[2]

Nevertheless, there can be little doubt that some suspicion of the King's motives began to form in the minds of many of the deputies at this stage. Within a few weeks this suspicion was to grow to a certainty that Louis XVI was not to be trusted.

In the meantime, on June 19th, the Clergy had decided, by a small majority, to join the Commons. On June 25th forty-seven nobles came over. As a result, the King two days later consented to the union of the three Orders. The battle of the *vote par tête* had been won.

A minority of the Nobility were to remain intractable. On July 4th they sent the following declaration to the Assembly:

The Order of the Nobility in the Estates General, whose members are accountable to their electors, to the entire nation, and to posterity for the use which they have made of the powers conferred upon them, and for the preservation of the principles which have been transmitted down to them from age to age by the French Monarchy, declare that they have never ceased to regard as inviolable and constitutional maxims the distinction and independence of the Orders, the *vote par ordre* and the royal sanction for all laws made in the Estates General.

This, however, was of little significance. The Assembly now included the majority of all three Orders; the King's recognition of the new status had been obtained. Henceforward, there appeared to be no obstacle to the work of the Assembly as a united whole.

Throughout the period of the deadlock, the Third Estate had received continuous support and encouragement, not only from the crowd of spectators which was in continuous attendance in the *Salle*

---

[1] J. S. Bailly, op. cit., Vol. I, p. 241.
[2] Ibid., p. 242.

des Menus Plaisirs, but from the increasingly influential *Club Breton*, which had established itself at Versailles from April 28th.[1]   Originally, the Club had been formed by the progressive Breton deputies to the Estates General to examine and co-ordinate the instructions laid down for them in their *cahiers*.   By the end of May, however, the Club had attracted to membership many of the more radical deputies from other parts of the country; many of the decisions reached in the Estates General by the deputies of the Third Estate had been thoroughly discussed and agreed on in advance in this Club.[2]   As early as May 3rd, the Club had pronounced itself in favour of the adoption of the second Article of the *cahier* from Rennes that the Third Estate, consisting of ninety per cent of the nation, had been termed an Order by mistake; that instead of being made a counterweight to the two privileged Orders, it should be renamed the 'People' or the 'Nation', with or without the adherence of the privileged Orders.[3]

On May 6th, on the motion of Delaville-Leroulx, the Club had opposed Malouet's suggestion that deputations should be sent to the Nobility and Clergy.   On May 12th, the speech made by Le Chapelier, to which we have already referred, was discussed and formulated in the Club.[4]   During the days which followed, almost every important decision reached by the deputies of the Commons in the Estates General was previously debated in the Club.[5]   Later, at the Jacobins in Paris, the influence of the Club was to become yet stronger.

Who, then, were the deputies who, from June 27th, were to undertake the task of formulating a new Constitution for their country? What shades of political opinion did they represent?   To answer this question adequately would need as many volumes as there were dominant personalities in the Assembly.   At the risk of doing less than justice to many of these men, and of anticipating much that follows in later chapters, it may, nevertheless, be helpful to outline, at this stage, the chief schools of political thought which existed in the Assembly in 1789, and to identify the leaders of each such school.   It must be emphasised that the growth of political groups in the Assembly was a gradual process, and at no time were such groups comparable with 'parties' in the English sense of the word.   They were made up of deputies who held differing views as to what was entailed by the Revolution.   From the extreme Right to the extreme Left, they were

---

[1] Bouchard, op. cit., pp. 21 f., Formation et Composition du Club.
[2] Ibid., p. 63, note.   [3] Ibid., p. 64.
[4] Ibid., p. 65.   [5] Ibid., pp. 66 f.

all anxious to stay the Revolution as soon as it had reached that point at which the political and social ends they deemed valid had been attained. That the forces which they had released in securing popular backing for the supremacy of the Third Estate were to prove too strong for them, that the momentum gained by the Revolution was to carry them beyond the point at which they wanted to stop, all this was to become apparent only as the years went by. In 1789, a triumphant Third Estate was to become aware quite soon that different groups of its members had different ideas, and that many of these ideas were quite irreconcilable. What, then, were these groups?

If the extremists of the Right Wing, such as the Vicomte de Mirabeau, d'Eprémesnil and other members of the First and Second Estates be excluded from consideration—men who had been compelled to join the Assembly against their convictions by the royal edict of June 27th; men whose sole anxiety was to preserve as much as possible of the *status quo ante* which was compatible with their own ambitions, and failing that, to attempt to discredit the new Assembly in every possible way—four, or possibly five, political groups are to be distinguished.

Primarily, there was to emerge fairly soon a group of deputies who were largely opposed to any revolutionary break in the French political system. Whilst admitting that under *l'ancien régime* political life had become corrupt, they believed that a purification of the existing governmental system by a removal of the usurpers from power would restore in full the ancient glory of the monarchy. They insisted that France could not be treated as one would treat a new country; it possessed a noble heritage of fourteen centuries of political experience, which must be taken into account by the constitution-making body.

Leading members of this group were Cazalès and the Abbé Maury. The latter seems to have been actuated largely by personal considerations. Vain and ambitious, he stood to gain from the preservation of *l'ancien régime*. He seems to have been more concerned about the possible loss of an annual income of some 20,000 livres than with the implications of a new political system. This was to lead to his insistence upon the inviolability of the clergy and the preservation of their ancient prerogatives. He appears to have hoped that his policy would sooner or later gain him the favour of Rome. 'I shall perish in the Revolution,' he is reported to have said, 'or, in fighting it, I shall gain the hat of a cardinal.'[1]

---

[1] A. Aulard : *Les Orateurs de la Révolution: l'Assemblée Constituante*, p. 220.

Cazalès was as sincere as the Abbé Maury was self-seeking.   An admirer of the English system of parliamentary government, of that country 'in which the nation is as free as the King is respected',[1] he was against the union of the three Estates, believing in particular that the Order of the Clergy was a necessary buffer between the Nobility and the Third Estate.   He dreamed of a monarchy which would take up an intermediary position between a royal despotism on the one hand and a parliamentary government on the other.   He believed that such a monarchy would protect the liberties of the people from attack by the Assembly, as the Assembly would preserve them from any arbitrary action on the part of the King.   Whilst admitting that all taxation should be controlled by the representatives of the people, he violently opposed every move in the Assembly to reduce the power and prerogatives of the Crown.

Montlosier and the Abbé de Montesquiou were lesser figures. They both feared the implications of the Revolution and were anxious to preserve much of the political structure of *l'ancien régime*.   Both deputies, however, were more liberal in outlook than the other members of their group, and as the months went by, they were not infrequently applauded by the Centre and Left for their moderation.   Such occasional periods of popularity were to enable the latter, for example, to secure the equal treatment of the Jesuits, proscribed before 1789, with that accorded to the other religious orders; whilst the former was to be quite capable of opposing his friend Cazalès over the question of the eligibility of deputies for election to the succeeding legislature. 'The case for proved ability is not necessarily conducive to the maintenance of liberty,' he was to assert.

A second group of deputies, of more liberal outlook than those of the Right Wing, were to form what may be called the Right Centre in the Assembly.   About thirty in number, their political outlook, which had been much influenced by Montesquieu's account of the English political system in his *L'Esprit des Lois*, tended to be moderate; their desire was to shift political power from the aristocracy to the wealthier bourgeoisie.   But this was all they desired.   Generally referred to as *Les Monarchiens* or *Les Impartiaux*, they were loyal supporters of the monarchy and of the existing religious order, and they were basically opposed to any expropriation of property right.   As the weeks went by, their fear of the masses was to grow rapidly; they were very anxious that no radical change should take place in the political and

[1] Mme de Staël: *Considérations*, Vol. II, p. 19.

social structure of the nation. They desired the establishment of a government based on the English system as they understood it, and to this end they were to insist upon the setting up of a bicameral legislature and upon the absolute right of veto of the King.

Realising, with their more liberal colleagues in the Assembly, the necessity for securing the continued support of the masses, they paid lip-service to such doctrines as those of natural liberty, popular sovereignty and the rights of man, but they remained anxious about their commitments in this respect. Malouet, a prominent member of the group, summed up its outlook as 'unable to tolerate any attack on *l'ancien régime*, as irritated by any innovation necessitated by circumstances as they would have been by a complete upheaval'.[1] In general their political creed envisaged reform, but not revolution.

Malouet's political views were moderate in the extreme. Elected by the Third Estate of the *sénéchaussée* of Riom to the Estates General in his absence, he was subsequently dismayed at the advanced political views of his constituents. 'I was on the point of sending in my resignation', he confessed, 'when I found the lesser bourgeoisie, lawyers and practitioners, without any knowledge of public affairs, quoting from *Le Contrat Social*, declaiming violently against tyranny and abuses, and each and every one proposing a Constitution.'[2] During the period of the deadlock in the Estates General, he had, whilst favouring the verification of powers in common, insisted upon awaiting the free consent to this process of the other two Orders. Later he had opposed the adoption of the title 'National Assembly', and he was to consider any Declaration of the Rights of Man to be little more than dangerous metaphysics. He was to be a supporter of bicameralism and of the absolute veto, and he founded the *Club des Impartiaux* to further the political views of his group.

Clermont-Tonnerre was another outstanding member of the group. He was an inveterate Anglophile and his views were pronounced with little regard for public opinion. His staunch advocacy of the absolute veto, for example, was later to imperil his life at the hands of the mob. He insisted that there had been a Constitution under *l'ancien régime*, a return to which, providing its true principles were applied, would prove a panacea for all political restiveness and avoid any necessity for revolutionary change.

A third member of the Monarchical Group was Mounier, who had

---

[1] *Mémoires*, Vol. II, p. 306.
[2] Ibid., Vol. I, p. 278.

achieved considerable political fame in his native province of Dauphiné before being unanimously elected by his constituents to the Estates General.   He, too, had been much influenced by Montesquieu and de Lolme; his enthusiasm for the English political system indeed, as described by these writers, had led to his learning the English language in order the better to understand it.   He was to prove a staunch advocate of a two-chambered legislature, of the absolute veto and of a strict separation of the powers of government.   He was jealous of the royal prerogative whilst supporting parliamentary institutions.   He it was who had proposed the oath of the tennis court.   Later, when he more fully realised the radical character of the political views of the great majority of the deputies, he was to repent the rôle he had played on June 20th, and so far to recant his opinions as to praise the conduct of Martin d'Auch, the one deputy who had refused to take the oath.

On October 10th, 1789, he was compelled to fly from the Parisian mob, and in Dauphiné, where in 1788 he had raised the standard of reform, he was now to attempt to raise the forces of counter-revolution. Exiled by the Assembly, the part he had played in the Revolution was to fill him with remorse.   Like Mirabeau, he was destined to be 'overwhelmed by the thought that all I have accomplished has been to help on a huge destruction'.

Lally-Tollendal was also a member of the Group of the Right Centre, but unlike most of its other members he was to retain his popularity both with the Assembly and with the mob.   This was partly due to his plain and precise manner of speech, to his emphatic use of everyday words and expressions.   He remained, however, as ardent a monarchist as any other member of his party.   He attributed the Revolution to the failure of the King's counsellors.   These once removed, all would be well![1]

Lesser members of the group were Bergasse, Virieu, Boufflers and d'Antraigues.   Although vociferous in the Assembly, they were to make no outstanding contribution to the politics of that body. D'Antraigues was to make his greatest speech in support of the royal veto.   Bergasse was to distinguish himself in his plan for the organisation of the judicial power.   They loyally supported their leaders, Virieu perhaps deserving special mention for his pronouncedly reactionary views.

It is important to emphasise, nevertheless, that the group recognised that the sovereign power in the State resided in the nation itself.   It

[1] Cf. Aulard, op. cit., p. 362.

was Mounier who was to formulate Article III of the Declaration of Rights, which read, 'The principle of sovereignty resides essentially in the nation. No body, no individual, can exert authority which does not expressly emanate therefrom.' In this, the party of the Right Centre were at one with those of the Left Centre and the Left Wing. But in order to prevent despotism, the exercise of the sovereign power, in their view, should necessarily be so divided that no one power of government might become too strong. In particular, the King was to preserve his full authority as the executive power in the nation, although the group, as we shall note later, was divided on the question as to whether or not he should form an integral part of the legislature.

The party of the Left Centre was to become the predominant group in the Assembly. It was to bear various names. Initially, when there was as yet little distinction between the political views of its members and those of the Left Wing proper, it shared with the latter their title of *Patriotes*. When Lafayette founded the *Club de 1789*, whose bourgeois character was preserved at the expense of a fairly high entry fee, they received the name of *Ministériels;* subsequently, when the Jacobin Club generally reflected their views, they became known as *Constitutionnels*, but later still they were to become identified with the *Feuillants* when the club of that name was opened after the massacre of the Champ de Mars.[1]

Whatever name the party bore, it was, in effect, the Constituent Assembly. Its members defended their moderate outlook against the deputies of the extreme Left, and their liberalism against the Right Wing groups. They represented a wider influence than the Monarchists, for they more truly reflected the views of the upper- and middle-class bourgeoisie, including such intellectuals as the lawyers and the leaders of the lesser clergy.

In 1789, the political outlook of the group differed from that of the Right Centre only in the matter of emphasis. More suspicious of the King, the Court and the ministers than were the Monarchists, they were not so ready to grant him real, as distinct from formal, power. During the following two years, as we shall see, this suspicion deepened and led to an increasing emphasis being placed by the group upon the power of the legislative body at the expense of that of the executive.

---

[1] Until 1791, the Jacobins was not a party club, although it tended to identify itself with the party of the Left Centre. After the flight of the King to Varennes, it adopted a republican outlook—hence the formation of the *Feuillants* by the Constitutional Group.

The political ideas of the Left Centre began more and more to resemble those advanced by Rousseau as the months went by, in contrast to the affinity of the Right Centre for those of Montesquieu. But a growing fear of the mob was constantly to remind them of the danger of going too far, and of permitting political control to pass from the hands of *la haute et la moyenne bourgeoisie*.

The leading members of the group were lawyers, such as Thouret, Tronchet, Le Chapelier, Target and d'André; ecclesiastics such as Sieyès and Grégoire; Jansenists like Camus and Martineau; noblemen who had identified themselves with the spirit of reform, including La Rochefoucauld, Montmorency, Beaumetz and Lafayette; municipal leaders such as Bailly, and journalists such as Barère.

The lawyers were to become prominent in their drafting of the minutiae of the Constitution. Thouret was to distinguish himself in connection with his proposals for the introduction of a jury system in criminal cases. Le Chapelier, in addition to being largely responsible for the formation of the National Guard of July 13th, 1789, also drafted the important laws of succession. He was to insist upon the election of the judges by popular vote. Target was to contribute largely to the plan for electoral reform and to draft many of the details of electoral procedure. Tronchet, a man of more than sixty years of age, was to give valuable assistance to the Committee on Feudalism, and to be prominent during the debates on the reorganisation of the judicial system.

D'André was destined to play a minor rôle in the Assembly until the time came for the Constitution to be revised in 1791. By this time his party had become anxious to stem as far as possible the progress which the Revolution was to show every sign of developing. But it was equally anxious to avoid the unpopularity which such a policy was to incur so far as the masses were concerned. It was d'André's fate to be the scapegoat thrust forward to bear the brunt of the storm.

Sieyès, Grégoire and Rabaut de St. Etienne were to play a more prominent part than did the lawyers in settling the main issues raised by the political outlook of their group, and in formulating the decisions of the Assembly.

Sieyès, whose famous pamphlet had been widely read before the meeting of the Estates General, was the great advocate in the Assembly of the system of representative democracy. To no small degree he was an original thinker. Influenced chiefly by Descartes, he believed in building up a political system from first principles, from *une table rase*.

He was critical of Montesquieu and asserted that politics was inevitably concerned with 'what should be' rather than with 'what is'. But equally he condemned Rousseau as 'a philosopher whose sensibilities were as perfect as his views were feeble'.[1]

Although many of his views had a republican flavour (in the modern sense of the word), he was to assert, even after the King's flight to Varennes, that 'I prefer a monarchy, because I am assured that there is more individual liberty for the citizen in a monarchy than in a republic.' As has been noted, it was Sieyès who had drawn up the motion which constituted the Third Estate as the National Assembly of France.

But as the months went by, Sieyès was fated to lose progressively his influence over the other members of his group. His particular draft of the new Constitution was not even to be discussed. He was to fail in his effort to secure the passage of a plan to establish a jury in civil as in criminal cases. His suggestions concerning the liberty of the press were to be given little consideration by the Assembly.

Nevertheless, Sieyès must be regarded as one of the chief architects of the Constitution of 1791. It was upon his plans for a representative democracy that the Assembly was to be enabled to build a Constitution in the primary interests of the upper and middle bourgeoisie without straining to breaking-point the teachings of the current philosophy.

The Abbé Grégoire was to become the advocate in the Assembly of the peasant, the *curé* and the humbler workman. He identified Christianity with social brotherhood. Thus, in the debate on the electoral system, he was to assert, 'To be an elector, or to be eligible for election to a primary assembly, it is sufficient that one be a good citizen, possessed of a sound judgment, and having a French heart.' In the light of these views, it cannot be a matter for surprise that he was to prove an opponent of the principle of royal inviolability.[2]

Grégoire was to become the idol of the lower clergy. Much of his political outlook was typical of that of the Left Wing rather than of that of the Constitutional Group. His republican outlook was at times to be veiled with difficulty. Nevertheless, he was to vote with

---

[1] 'Que dire', he is reported to have said, 'si l'on voyait dans un autre genre de mécaniciens entreprendre le radoub ou la construction d'un vaisseau avec la seule théorie, avec les seules ressources des sauvages dans la construction de leurs pirogues?' On Sieyès, see especially P. Bastid: *Sieyès et sa Pensée* (Paris, 1939).

[2] On Grégoire see especially A. Gazier: *Etudes sur l'Histoire Religieuse de la Révolution*, in particular pp. 29 to 75.

his group on all major issues, for he believed that its programme was best suited to the needs of the day.

Rabaut de St. Etienne was a popular figure and a brilliant orator. He was the third great member of the Clergy who ornamented the ranks of the Left Centre. Apart from a magnificent speech in favour of religious freedom, he was not, however, to be responsible for any particular political development in the Assembly. A sincere liberal, he was devoted to the principles established by his party; in 1791 he was to be numbered amongst those deputies who were under the delusion that with the King's signature to the Constitution, the Revolution was accomplished. Today he would be described as a good party man, who could be entrusted to reinforce with his eloquence the proposals made by his leaders.

The Jansenists supported the doctrine of the equality of men. Hence, to Camus, the King was no more than a man, and in office an official who required watching. Their main influence was to lie in the religious reforms which the Constituents endeavoured to carry out. The Civil Constitution of the Clergy was largely influenced by their ideas; they may therefore be charged with partial responsibility for the counter-revolution.

The noblemen were not responsible for any outstanding political contribution to the programme of their group. Montmorency, for example, was almost invariably to follow the lead of Sieyès; Beaumetz was to be the rapporteur of the Committee on Criminal Jurisprudence; Lafayette's sole significant contribution to the work of the Assembly was to lie in his presentation of a draft Declaration of the Rights of Man. He deserves mention rather because of his picturesque character than because of any contribution he was destined to make to the Constitution of 1791. His participation in the American War of Independence had given him an enthusiasm for liberty, social equality and a limited monarchy. He it was who inaugurated the National Guard in June, 1789, a bourgeois undertaking designed to keep the Fourth Estate in its rightful place. His *bête noire* was to be Mirabeau, who was frequently to attempt, and as often to fail, to secure his co-operation in his tortuous negotiations with the Court. Lafayette was enough of a soldier to realise the effect on Paris of that removal of the Court from Versailles to Rouen which Mirabeau was to become so anxious to bring about. He dreaded a civil war.

Bailly was the first President of the National Assembly. He was a distinguished scientist who had taken a prominent part in the municipal politics of Paris, of which city he had become Mayor. He was to make little contribution to the political ideas of his group. His age and his distinction, as well as his mayoralty, were to pick him out as one of the leaders of the Assembly.

Other members of the Left Centre included Goupil de Préfeln, Roederer, Dupont de Nemours, Regnaud, Treilhard, Merlin, Defermont, Boissy d'Anglas and Desmeuniers. In combination, they were to ensure that the political ideas of the upper- and middle-class bourgeoisie gained ascendancy in the Assembly. They subscribed to the technique of thought by which the Constitution of 1791 was established, a technique which will be examined in detail in subsequent chapters.

A smaller group of deputies, whose politics were scarcely removed from those of the Left Centre, but who deserve to be distinguished because of a certain independence of thought which they were to develop, was the so-called Triumvirate, which took its name from its three leaders Barnave, Alexandre de Lameth and Adrien Duport, although the group was actually to embrace some thirty to forty deputies which included Charles de Lameth, the Duc d'Aiguillon, Menou and Beauharnais.

Adrien Duport was a deputy who had been elected by the nobility of Paris, and he had been one of the first members of his Order to make common cause with the Third Estate during the period of the deadlock. His chief claim to fame was to lie in his scheme for the reorganisation of the judiciary, which he was to present to the Assembly in 1790.

The accepted leader of the group, however, was Barnave, whose *Introduction à la Révolution Française*, written in prison, was to prove one of the most important of all the revolutionary documents. Throughout his life he was suspicious of pure theory. He had a complete contempt for those 'who profess metaphysical ideas, largely because they have no ideas of their own; who envelop all about them with clouds of theory, because they are fundamentally ignorant of any knowledge of government in the real world'. He had a great admiration for the political systems of both England and America, but he nevertheless remained in outlook a realist.[1] He was to support the right of the King to veto acts of the legislature, and although he favoured a bicameral assembly, he yet was to find it expedient to vote

[1] Cf. Boissenot: *Les Opinions Politiques de Barnave* (Paris, Thesis, 1919), esp. pp. 59 f.

for a single chamber. For he was to conclude that France could not copy England in this matter, as in the latter country the peers of the realm were remote from the mass of the people and so were capable of independent judgment, whilst in France not only had there been no clear distinction between *la haute* and *la petite noblesse*, but the events of July 14th were to be, in his view, sufficient to render all Frenchmen equal.

On the other hand, he did not believe it possible to emulate America, where there were no class distinctions at all. A second chamber, elected on the American system, would, he considered, serve merely to perpetuate those undesirable distinctions which had been so pronounced a feature of *l'ancien régime*.

It was Barnave who was to be largely responsible for steering the Assembly through the difficult waters which were increasingly to separate the philosophical ideals of the century from the narrower political opportunism which was so soon to be employed to safeguard the interests of the bourgeoisie as distinct from those of the nation as a whole. A brilliant orator, it was said of him by Camille Desmoulins that 'in the most important debates in the National Assembly, it is always M. Barnave's speech which is kept for the grand finale, and the debate always ends after he has spoken'.

Barnave's greatest speech was possibly to be that on the inviolability of the King. In one of his last speeches in the Assembly, he was to oppose Robespierre's motion to exclude existing deputies from the subsequent legislature, the acceptance of which was to prove one of the most fatal mistakes of the Constituent Assembly.

The extreme Left Wing in the Assembly was composed of democrats whose political views were republican rather than monarchical in character. For them the sovereign power in the State was finally vested in the legislature. The executive and subsidiary powers of government were, in their view, no more than functions of government, subjected at all times to the over-riding authority of the Assembly. Hence they were critical of the monarchy, and anxious at all times to limit its power. They were to insist that the clauses of the Declaration of Rights should be fully implemented, so as to give full effect to the doctrine of the sovereignty of the people. They were, for example, to oppose bitterly any restriction of the suffrage. As a group, the Left Wing represented the interests of the smaller proprietor and business man, of the rank and file of the professional classes, of the *petite bourgeoisie* generally. They respected property right, and were far from being socialist in outlook, although they favoured greater equality of status and opportunity amongst individual men and women.   This group of deputies was to have little influence upon the course of events prior to the flight to Varennes, which, however, was an event in itself fully corroborative of the group's earlier misgivings.

The group included Robespierre, Pétion de Villeneuve, Buzot, Prieur de la Marne and Reubell.   A certain inflexibility of purpose, an adherence to a strict interpretation of the Declaration of Rights, a distaste for compromise, qualities which earned for Robespierre the title of 'The Incorruptible', were indeed generally characteristic of them all.

Pétion's claim to fame was to be chiefly based on his persistent fight for the full implementation of the letter of the Declaration of Rights. Buzot was to be known for his unique suggestion that the legislature should be divided by lot into two sections, in each of which separate discussion should take place; in this way he tried to meet the objection of the bicameralists that a single-chambered legislature would fail to provide against the dangers of hasty or unwise legislation.

But, in general, the members of the group supported Robespierre's political views, which in turn were greatly influenced by the teachings of Rousseau's *Le Contrat Social*.   They believed that they were called upon to legislate not only in the interests of France, but in those of all humanity.   Their outlook was international; the scope of their ideas universal.   On May 17th, 1791, Duport was to reproach Robespierre with having uninterruptedly held a chair of natural law since the inception of the Assembly, the occupation of which he had usurped to himself.

Robespierre was destined not to distinguish himself as a member of the Constituent Assembly.   His time had not yet come.   Throughout its life, he was to give the impression of being a man who could afford to wait, who saw further than his colleagues and was fully aware that the Revolution had scarcely begun.

His popularity with the mob was to date from the time of his violent opposition to the King's right of absolute veto.   As the months went by, the Assembly was to treat him with increasing respect, and he was to be successful in getting two motions approved by this body.   The first was one preventing any member of the Assembly from accepting ministerial office, a motion principally directed against Mirabeau. The second was to prevent any existing member of the Assembly from being elected to the following Legislative Assembly. It was in the Jacobin Club, rather than in the Assembly, that Robespierre was to lay the foundations of his future power.

Finally there was Mirabeau, who cannot readily be attached to any one of the political groups in the Assembly. It is not possible to say he had a settled policy. He was rather unscrupulous, adapting his views to the pressure of circumstances. Generally, he seems to have favoured a 'mixed system', a State in which was to be preserved all that was best in *l'ancien régime* whilst at the same time embodying as much as was expedient of the new democratic liberalism.

He was ambitious for power. Contemptuous of theory, particularly of the views expressed in the *Contrat Social*, he was to find illimitable scope for his talents in attempting to reconcile the current concept of popular sovereignty with the older concept of the sovereignty of the King—two ideas which were irreconcilable. His magnificent powers of oratory were to make him a leader in the Assembly where, according to Madame de Campan, he resembled an Atlas. Had he lived, he may have brought his ideas to fruition by establishing a constitutional government and saving the monarchy. As it was, he was to fail to shake the principles of the Constitutional Party. Thus, for example, his opposition to the plan for a Declaration of Rights was to come to nothing. Mirabeau was essentially an opportunist, with one foot in the Assembly and one in the circles of the Court. Perhaps he was the only man who could have reconciled the two. His death, in April, 1791, meant that the Constitutionalists, despite the flight of the King shortly afterwards, were to be enabled to complete the Constitution without further serious opposition.

These, then, were the men who were to be responsible for the legislation of the first two years of the Revolution, and for the implementation of the demand of the nation for popular sovereignty. It is again necessary to insist that the political outlook of the groups outlined above did not represent the 'cut-and-dried' policies of clearly defined parties in 1789. Such policies represented the gradual evolution of the political thought of the deputies as it was to be moulded by the events of the months which followed the meeting of the Estates General. In 1789 there was one Third Estate, enthusiastic, idealistic, conscious that it represented the nation as against the privileged classes, ready to conform to the tenets of the current *mystique*. But under the pressure of events, this idealism was to fade. The democrats were to become suspicious of the Monarchists; they were to view with growing suspicion the vacillations of the King, the activities of the *émigrés* and the departure of members from the Assembly. In turn, the Monarchists were to become increasingly hostile to the Left Wing. They feared the mob, and suspected that the deputies of the Left were manœuvring to prepare the way for a republic.

In the meantime, the Centre Party was to occupy itself with the perpetuation of the Revolution until the bourgeoisie had entered into their kingdom by attaining their rightful place in the scheme of things. They were then prepared to arrest its progress, and with this end in view, they were to prove increasingly willing to sacrifice the revolutionary ideals to the interests of their own class.

Perhaps Robespierre alone was really sincere in his political convictions. In 1791, a portrait of him exhibited in the Salon bore the title 'The Incorruptible'. But by this time the Jacobins were already laying their plans to keep the Revolution alive. The nation was swinging to the Left, and it was already becoming clear that far from being accomplished, the Revolution was as yet but gaining momentum.

CHAPTER I

THE DECLARATION OF RIGHTS

THE constitutional work of the National Assembly was destined to begin in an atmosphere of suspicion, mistrust and fear. Primarily there was fear and mistrust of the King, and suspicion of the activities of the Ministry and of the Court. The vacillating character of Louis XVI, reflected in his apparent readiness to countermand orders which he had given upon the slightest hint of resistance to the royal will, had caused much uneasiness amongst the members of the Assembly. On June 27th, for example, the King, bowing before the will of the Third Estate, had rescinded his four-day-old command to the Estates General to separate and carry on their discussions *par ordre*, and, completely reversing this decision, had ordered the Nobility and Clergy to join the Third Estate in the *Salle des Menus Plaisirs*. This represented a no mean victory for the Commons. But it was an uneasy victory. Would the King change his mind again?

The deputies were not long to be left in doubt. Almost immediately, Louis was to regret the decision he had taken. Under the reactionary influence of his closest advisers, he seems to have decided overnight to restore the pre-existing order by resort, if necessary, to armed force. Arthur Young records that on July 9th, as he was travelling to Châlons 'through a poor country and poor crops', he met a regiment whose officer told him that 'they were on the way to Paris, that Maréchal Broglie was appointed to command an army of 50,000 men near Paris—it was necessary—the Tiers-Etat was running mad —and wanted some wholesale correction—they wanted to establish a republic—absurd'.[1] By July 11th, some twenty regiments were strategically placed between Versailles and Paris—between the 'sovereign people' and its chosen representatives.

On this day, the King struck his blow. Necker was dismissed, and replaced by the reactionary Baron de Breteuil, whose job was to collaborate with de Broglie to restore the position and bring the rebellious Commons to order. Paris was frightened and infuriated. Since May 18th the city had been largely controlled by some four

[1] *Travels in France and Italy* (Everyman ed.), pp. 158, 159.

hundred electors whose duty had been to elect the Paris deputies to the Estates General. Thereafter, instead of dispersing, they had retained a watching brief, become a body of administrators, virtually replacing the existing municipal government and playing no small part in reinforcing the stand of the Third Estate against the King. Throughout this period, they had acted as a central committee, providing the revolutionary elements in the city with a directional nucleus.

The effect of the massing of troops and the dismissal of Necker upon the citizens of Paris, the sequence of events which led up to the capture of the Bastille, is well known. Urged on by the orators of the Palais Royal, on that day Paris saved the Assembly and perpetuated the Revolution. Fearing for the loyalty of the troops, and indecisive as ever, Louis made his second capitulation to the Commons within a period of three weeks. Not only did he disperse his troops and reinstate Necker, but he came to the Assembly on the morning of July 15th to announce this capitulation in person. Two days later, he made a state visit to Paris where, at the Hôtel de Ville, he wore the tricolour and was enthusiastically hailed by the crowd as 'Father of the French, King of a Free People'. As Bailly, standing as President of the Assembly instead of kneeling as Mayor of Paris, remarked, 'On this day the People has reconquered its King.'

Nevertheless, there can be no doubt that the unpredictable attitude of the King, despite this apparent acquiescence in the events of the Revolution, led to a perpetuation of the atmosphere of distrust and uncertainty in the Assembly. As Sagnac has emphasised, Louis lacked both will-power and political sense. Surrounded by irresolute ministers in whom he had no confidence, he became more and more timid. He formulated no plan. He shirked his responsibilities. At one moment he meditated flight. At another he appeared to be reconciled to the new state of affairs.

This mistrust of the King, the Court and the Ministry, which continued throughout the period of office of the Constituent Assembly, was to have a powerful influence upon the evolution of the idea of popular sovereignty, which was to be the starting-point of the constitutional legislation of the Assembly. Almost every important constitutional decision was destined to be at least partly the result of some reactionary move on the part of the King.[1]

[1] Cf. Deslandres: *Histoire Constitutionnelle de la France,* Vol. I, pp. 63 f. He particularly emphasises that the real reason for the formulation of the Declaration was the desire of the Assembly to secure a safeguard against the return of absolutism (p. 71).

But an equally potent factor which influenced the Assembly, which has received much less attention from historians, was a growing fear among the deputies of the potential influence of the Paris mob, with its twin centres of political direction—the Hôtel de Ville and the Palais Royal. By no means negligible at Versailles, this influence was to become of greater significance when the Assembly moved to Paris. From the outset, the mob had mingled freely with deputies in the *Salle des Menus Plaisirs*. It had no hesitation in roaring its disapproval of the speeches made by members of the extreme Right Wing, as often of the more moderate counsels of the Monarchists. As early as June, 1789, the deputies of the Nobility and the higher Clergy had been hustled, insulted and occasionally maltreated on entering and leaving the Assembly. Any opposition to the more revolutionary motions proposed by the Left, any defence of the attitude of the King or of the privileged Orders, aroused catcalls and threats in the Assembly itself, the names of the offending deputies being listed and later publicised and denounced in the popular clubs which were rapidly formed from 1789 onwards, as also in the Palais Royal, and such speakers were invariably blacklisted in the revolutionary journals. On one occasion a particular motion was initially opposed by some 300 deputies. Under pressure of visitors to the Assembly, the opposition was decreased to 90 deputies, and finally to one, and he was compelled to escape by an unguarded door. As Malouet remarked, on July 14th the reign of terror had already begun. De Ferrières wrote, 'Liberty has ceased to exist, even in the National Assembly itself.'[1] The property, the families and even the lives of the deputies of the Right were frequently in danger.

Many deputies refused to remain in the Assembly. Taine estimated that from five to six hundred deputies had procured their passports by October, 1789, and that one hundred and twenty had already left. By the end of this month, such leading deputies as Mounier, Lally-Tollendal and the Bishop of Langres had left Paris. It is therefore clear that in assessing the political outlook of the Assembly, due account must be taken of this direct influence upon the deputies. The particular development which was to characterise the evolution of the concept of popular sovereignty during the years 1789–91 owed not a little to the twin fears of the King and his Ministers on the one hand, and of the populace on the other.

Under these circumstances, it was a matter of urgent necessity for the Assembly to consolidate its position, to establish its authority upon

[1] *Mémoires*, Vol. I, p. 168.

a *de jure* basis in place of a *de facto* seizure of power. The problem which faced the Assembly was how to establish the Constitution upon a foundation at once older and more fundamental than existing political right and historic privilege. The overthrow of the existing order, and the implementation of the principle of popular sovereignty, could be justified only by an appeal to first principles, to a system of rights of universal validity, emerging from an original 'natural order of things' in whose name the existing political framework could be swept aside. Historic right had necessarily to be subordinated to natural right, divine right to the right of the sovereign nation.

It was this necessity for establishing the legal basis of its authority which caused the Assembly to decide upon the formulation of a Declaration of the Rights of Man. Such a decision was easier to reach by virtue of the fact that such a Declaration had been demanded by a majority of the *cahiers* which had reached Versailles; indeed, Clermont-Tonnerre pointed out that the question of a Declaration of Rights was the only one upon which a division of opinion was discernible.

It is probable that no political event in the Revolution has given rise to more speculation and controversy than that of the Declaration of Rights of August, 1789. Its origins have been traced to a multitude of sources. Its significance has variously been found to lie in its codification of so-called natural rights which either protect the individual against the State or the people against a despotic monarch; in its being a charter at once determining and limiting the rights conferred by membership of the State upon the individuals composing it, and yet again in its being little more than a list of the fundamental liberties of man which would serve as a guide alike to citizen and statesman in the new political order.

Janet, whilst admitting that the immediate origin of the Declaration lay in the American Bills of Rights, as also in the clauses of the Declaration of Independence itself, was convinced that it was French political thought by which the American legislators had been inspired. 'We must not forget', he wrote, 'that France herself played a considerable part in the American Revolution . . . that the theory of the Rights of Man was a completely French theory, which had been declared by our philosophers of the eighteenth century, by Voltaire, Montesquieu, Rousseau and Turgot, and that it was from us that it passed to America.'[1] Later, he attributed the origin of the American ideas more specifically to Rousseau. 'As for the Declaration itself,' he

---

[1] *Histoire de la Science Politique,* Intro. to 3rd. ed., pp. xxxv f.

added, 'is it other than a contract made between all the members of the community, according to Rousseau's ideas? Is it more than the enunciation of the clauses and conditions of this contract?'[1] An answer to this question was provided by Jellinek. After stating that it was difficult to believe that an author so familiar with the *Contrat Social* could have perpetrated such a mistake, he went on to show that 'the principles of the *Contrat Social* are absolutely contrary to any Declaration of Rights; for from them flow, not the rights of the individual, but the power of the "general will" which juridically is limitless'.[2] His conclusion was that 'the French have not only adopted the ideas of the Americans, but also the form in which these were expressed on the other side of the Atlantic'. He showed that the Americans, in turn, had been inspired by the works of Locke and of Blackstone. But as we shall see below, Jellinek also was mistaken as to the identity which he believed to exist between the American and French Declarations.

Faguet had no doubt that Montesquieu was indirectly responsible for the Declaration. 'Montesquieu', he wrote, 'laid down the basis for the Declaration of the Rights of Man, and was responsible for its essential characteristics . . . he, more than any one, inspired it.'[3] Fabre, on the other hand, favoured Locke's philosophy as being the true fount of the Declaration.[4]

Emile Boutmy supported Janet's conclusions. He found that the French Declaration gave him 'the feeling of Rousseau', he felt that it was 'Rousseau *tout pur*'.[5] Marcaggi, however, whilst concurring in general with the thesis advanced by Jellinek, traced the origin of the Declaration more specifically to the Physiocrats, and concluded that even without American precedent to guide them, Frenchmen would have been led inevitably to the Declaration of 1789.[6]

Champion favoured Voltaire as the source of the Declaration.[7] Taine,[8] Aulard,[9] Cole[10] and Herriot[11] may be numbered amongst other

[1] *Histoire de la Science Politique*, Vol. II, p. 457.
[2] *La Déclaration des Droits de l'Homme et du Citoyen*, pp. 10–12 f.
[3] *Politique Comparée de Montesquieu, Rousseau et Voltaire*, p. 281.
[4] *Les Pères de la Révolution*, p. 40.
[5] Article in *Annales des Sciences Politiques* of July, 1902, reproduced in *Etudes Politiques*, p. 224.
[6] *Les Origines de la Déclaration des Droits de l'Homme*, 1789, p. 224.
[7] *Rousseau et la Révolution Française*, pp. 121 (note), 122
[8] *L'Ancien Régime*, pp. 321 f.
[9] *Histoire Politique de la Révolution Française*, p. 23.
[10] Introduction to Everyman ed. of '*The Social Contract*', p. xxxvii.
[11] *Aux Sources de la Liberté*, p. 17.

writers of distinction who have reached conflicting conclusions concerning its origin.

Whilst noting the conflicting opinions of so many different writers, it is necessary to emphasise that both the form and content of the French Declaration are explicable ultimately only in terms of the particular political atmosphere in which it was drawn up. And this atmosphere was charged with that idea of sovereignty which was prevalent in the minds of a majority of the deputies at the time. Consideration of the Declaration from this point of view throws, as we shall see, new light upon the particular form in which it was finally codified.

Primarily, there can be no doubt that its inception was due to the determination of the Committee set up on July 11th to arrange the constitutional work of the Assembly, that 'in order to ensure the soundness of any Constitution, it is essential to found it on the Rights of Man, which, in turn, it should protect'; to a desire, as Volney said, 'to seek out with painstaking care what is the goal, what are the principles of all associations; to discover the rights which each member has therein, both the rights which he gives up and the rights which he must keep'. Such a view was confirmed by the first Constitutional Committee which, established on July 14th, made its first report to the Assembly on July 27th.

The composition of this Committee is interesting.[1] It was predominantly monarchist, having as members Champion de Cicé, Mounier, Bergasse, Lally-Tollendal and Clermont-Tonnerre, who outnumbered the remaining and more radical deputies Talleyrand, Sieyès and Le Chapelier. This itself is evidence of the original influence of the more moderate group in the Assembly, although the presence of three of the most active members of the Left Centre indicates a by no means negligible influence of the more extreme members.

Despite differences in their political views, this Committee agreed unanimously upon the urgent necessity for the formulation of a Declaration of Rights, and this view was communicated to the full Assembly on July 27th by its *rapporteur*, Champion de Cicé. There ensued a lively debate upon the necessity for such a Declaration. The majority of the deputies were anxious that the work of the Assembly should be placed on a constitutional basis. Distrust of the King and of the Ministry was the driving force. It was necessary to codify the

[1] Cf. Delagrange: *Le Premier Comité de Constitution de la Constituante.*

natural rights of man, to identify the constitutional ideas of the Assembly with the leading tenets of the current *mystique*, that *puissance anonyme et demi-inorganique* which, as we shall see, was to play so important a part in shaping the Constitution during the two following years.

The Declaration was therefore based on philosophical ideas which had become familiar to the masses as a series of *clichés*. Mounier claimed that it was necessary, to ensure a sound constitution, that the rights which natural justice had accorded to all citizens should be well known; it was necessary to recall the principles which formed the basis of all societies. In his view, every article of the Constitution should be the direct consequence of such a principle. Lafayette, in turn, insisted that the sentiments which nature had engraved on the heart of each individual should be publicised. Only in such a way would the nation come to love liberty by first recognising it. A Declaration of Rights would thus 'express the eternal truths from which all institutions should flow', and become a faithful guide which would serve constantly to remind the people of the source of their social and natural rights.

Durand de Maillane thought that a people which had lost its rights should know the principles on which they were to be re-established. The Comte de Castellane believed that men blinded by ignorance would do no more than change their fetters; he traced the source of all human misery to the prevailing ignorance of the natural rights of man, which could be removed only by their publication. Barnave considered man's knowledge of his natural rights an essential preliminary to the law-making process. He found that such a Declaration, apart from educating the public, would serve two other useful purposes— that of 'fixing the spirit of legislation, so that it would remain unimpaired for all time', and that of 'ensuring that such a spirit would animate the fulfilment of the laws'.

Desmeuniers held that a Declaration of Rights was necessary 'to fix the ideas of the people on the emanation of the principles of all societies'. Mirabeau asserted that ignorance or forgetfulness of, or contempt for, the natural rights of man were the sole cause of public misery and of the corruption of governments. These rights should be re-established in a solemn Declaration, as inalienable, imprescriptible and sacred, in order that such a statement of them might constantly remind all members of the social body of them.

Many more similar opinions were expressed. But as the days went by, the background against which the debate was carried on grew steadily darker. From the middle of July there was a disturbing extension of that wave of lawlessness which had been engendered by the fall of the Bastille. Impatient of the law-making process, the peasantry had determined to recover their rights by force. There was bloodshed at Cluny. At Mâcon twenty peasants were illegally hanged for failure to pay tithes and feudal dues. Such actions provoked further disorders. Ultimately a wave of terror swept the country. Exhortation having had little effect, the Assembly decided upon repression. A National Guard had been formed in July, carefully recruited from the bourgeois classes. At Lyons, it killed eighty rioters and took sixty prisoners. Law-officers travelled round Dauphiné, executing the guilty. Everywhere the bourgeoisie sympathised with the policy of repression. Ultimately the riots were quelled. What is important, however, was the effect of these disturbances in the Assembly.

As we have seen, there had already been some fear of the Parisian mob. The trouble in the provinces increased this fear and resulted in the growth of some considerable opposition to the project of a Declaration. This came largely from the Right Wing in the Assembly, although there was no small volume of support from the moderates in the party of the Right Centre. These deputies were increasingly fearful of the effects of the publication of such a Declaration in view of the lawless state of the country.

This opposition took three main forms. Primarily, there were deputies, amongst whom may be numbered Malouet, the Vicomte de Mirabeau, Champion de Cicé and La Luzerne, who had become totally opposed to the formulation of such a Declaration at all. They based their opposition on three main contentions. Initially, they insisted that the mass of the people were not in a fit state to understand the implications of such a Declaration, and that its publication would spread ideas which would be certain to be misunderstood and which would thus add to the prevailing lawlessness. 'Take note, gentlemen,' said Malouet, 'that there is not one of these natural rights which will not be modified in practice by the law. Let us suppose that in this conception of rights we take no account of what is, and that all the forms of government are free instruments in our hands; as soon as we have chosen one of them, instantly natural man and his rights will be modified. Why, then, begin by transporting him to the summit of a high mountain, and showing him his empire without limits, when he must descend to find them with every step he takes?'

Further, they were opposed to any intermixing of principles with the laws themselves. The former they considered to necessitate 'the conviction of man's reason', the latter 'the voluntary submission of man's will'. Lastly, to clinch their argument, they pointed out that any imitation of the American Bills of Rights was mistaken. American example was not conclusive. In that country there were no feudal complications. Luxury and indigence alike were absent; all were proprietors. Many developments were necessary and much time must elapse before men in France could be told they were equals.

A second form of opposition came from a group of deputies, including the Duc de Lévis and De Landine, who whilst agreeing that a Declaration of Rights was desirable, believed that it should not be formulated until the Constitution itself had been completed, and that it should then appear as an appendix drawn up in the light of the principles laid down in the Constitution. Malouet later identified himself with this point of view.

Finally, a third group of deputies were of the opinion that any such Declaration should include the duties, as well as the rights, of the individual citizen. This proposal was defeated on August 4th by no more than 570 votes to 433, largely as a result of the news which reached the deputies on that day of the outbreak of further trouble due to mob violence at Saint-Germain, at Pontoise and in Burgundy and Normandy.

The formulation of a Declaration of Rights being finally agreed upon, the Assembly was deluged in the days which followed by an embarrassingly large number of projected Declarations. As Lally-Tollendal remarked, 'Not a deputy had an idea but he needs must express it, not an opinion but he found it necessary to expound it from the tribune'. So many speakers were anxious to mount the tribune that Bouche facetiously demanded that an hour glass be placed upon the President's desk, and each speaker interrupted after five minutes. The Vicomte de Mirabeau proposed to avoid all further discussion by proposing that, instead of a Declaration, there should be placed at the head of the Constitution a simple statement such as, 'For the good of each and of all, we have decreed the following. . . .'

Ultimately, some thirty bureaux were empanelled to produce draft Declarations. On August 13th a Committee of Five, of which Mirabeau was rapporteur, was appointed to consider these various projects, and it decided in favour of that submitted by the Sixth Bureau[1] as a basis for subsequent discussion.

It is not possible here to follow the debates of the two following weeks in detail. Slowly the Declaration took form, the first three Articles ultimately decreed being proposed by Mounier. After declaring that men were born free and with equal rights, and that the end of their political association was the preservation of their natural, inalienable rights, Article Three decreed that the principle of all sovereignty resided in the nation. Thus the Assembly laid down the basis for the subsequent development of its theory of popular sovereignty.

Article Four, which defined liberty and the limits within which each man was free to enjoy the exercise of his rights, and Article Five, defining the boundaries of the law, were proposed by De Lameth. Article Six, which significantly defined the law as 'the expression of the general will', was drawn up by Talleyrand. The remaining Articles dealt largely with matters arising out of the first six Articles; several of them, indeed, could scarcely be called 'rights' at all.

Together with their declaration that the sovereign power was vested in the nation, the Assembly also emphasised that the law was the expression of the 'general will' of the nation. The significance of these twin decrees cannot be over-estimated. The Declaration of Rights as a whole cannot be understood without a proper appreciation of their peculiar relationship the one to the other, a relationship which was destined to become the *motif* of the Constitution which was slowly to emerge during the two ensuing years.

In order to understand this significance, however, it is first necessary to institute a careful comparison between the American Bills of Rights and the Declaration of Rights of the Constituent Assembly.

That the draft Declaration of the Sixth Bureau, as amended by the Assembly, was based on the American Bills there can be no doubt. The careful analysis of the various American codes with that of France which has been made by Jellinek,[2] places this direct influence beyond

---

[1] The Bureau included Champion de Cicé, the Comte de Montmorency, Anson, Laflore (Bishop of Nancy) and La Poule. Other notable drafts were those associated with Sieyès (*A.P.*, Vol. VIII, p. 458), Bouche (p. 438), Lafayette and Mirabeau.

[2] Op. cit., Chap. V. Cf. Faÿ, *L'Esprit Revolutionnaire en France et aux Etats-Unis à la fin du XVIIIe siècle*, p. 267. 'It seems therefore that the discussion may be considered closed. From the historical as well as from the ideological point of view, we have proofs that the Declaration of the Rights of Man, drawn up by the French Constitutional Assembly, was suggested and continually influenced by the examples of America.'

all reasonable doubt. The leading characteristic of the American Bills of Rights, whether we take that of Virginia, or Massachusetts, or Pennsylvania, or of any other State published prior to 1789[1] by way of example, was their insistence not only upon the existence of natural rights, founded upon the inalienable title of man as man to security of his life, his property and his liberty, but more important still, their recognition of the principle that the existence of these rights outside the State limited the power and authority of the State itself.[2]

Jellinek proved conclusively that the influence of Locke and of Blackstone was responsible in no small measure for this particular point of view developed by the American legislators.   In seeking, however, to show that the French Declaration embodied a similar idea, and in thereby attempting to destroy the thesis that the Declaration of 1789 was based on the political ideas of Rousseau, he made his great mistake. In his endeavour to prove the influence of Locke's philosophical thought upon the Constituent Assembly he was concerned to prove the common origin of American and French political thought in this matter.   In fact, although dispute has raged since his day on the origin of these various documents, it is safe to say that so successfully did he compare the French Declaration, clause by clause, with the American Bills that no one has seriously challenged his claim to have proved their identity in form.

But, in fact, the mistake made by Jellinek was that he failed to realise the subtle, but nevertheless fundamental, distinction between the French and American Declarations.   The distinction lies in the different view taken in either country of the extent of the power of the State.   Primarily it may be agreed that the content of natural rights in either case was similar.   Virginia defined these rights as 'the enjoyment of life and liberty, with the means of acquiring and possessing property, and pursuing and obtaining happiness and safety'. Massachusetts listed them more simply as 'life, liberty and property'. In France we find them as *la liberté, la propriété, la sûreté et la résist-*

[1] Notably Maryland (1776), North Carolina (1776), Vermont (1777) and New Hampshire (1784).
[2] The influence of Locke was profound. 'A man', he wrote, 'cannot subject himself to the arbitrary power of another; and having, in the state of nature, no arbitrary power over the life, liberty and possessions of another, but only so much as the law of nature gave him for the preservation of himself and the rest of mankind, this is all he doth, or can, give up to the commonwealth, and by it to the legislative power, so that the legislative power can have no more than this.'   (*On Civil Government.* Book II, Chap. IX.)   This principle is written into all the American Bills of Rights.

ance à l'oppression. In America generally such rights were to be enforced by standing laws which would 'secure the individuals composing the body politic in their power of enjoying, in safety and tranquillity, their natural rights and the blessings of life'. Hence the implication that such rights were pre-social in character and that it was the duty of the State to protect and enforce them.

But note the French attitude. The limits (upon the enjoyment of these rights) 'can be determined only by the State'. There is no mention of limitation in the American parallels. The French implication is that there are not only limits, but that the rights themselves are to be circumscribed and determined by the 'general will' of the nation.

Throughout the remaining Articles of the French and the various American Declarations the distinction is clear. Thus, for example, the Virginian Bill of Rights stated, 'The freedom of the press is one of the greatest bulwarks of liberty, and can never be restrained but by despotic governments.' That of Pennsylvania declared that 'the people have a right to freedom of speech and of writing and publishing their sentiments'. There is no limitation imposed upon this right. But in the French Declaration, '*Tout citoyen peut donc parler, écrire, imprimer librement sauf à répondre de l'abus de cette liberté dans les cas déterminés par la loi.*'

Such differences, superficially slight, are nevertheless fundamental. The State, as viewed by the Assembly in France, remained the final arbiter as to what rights men possessed. In America, the State was regarded as existing to enforce pre-existing rights, by which equally its powers were limited. But in France such rights were subject to the law, and the law was expressly defined as the 'general will' of the nation, which in practice could mean only the will of that body of men capable of determining such a 'general will'.

Such an interpretation of the implications of the French Declaration is reinforced by an examination of the debates which immediately preceded its promulgation. The growing tendency to insist upon the subordination of the natural rights of men to the authority of the 'general will' is reflected again and again in the speeches of deputies. On August 1st, for example, De Crénières claimed that man in the state of nature was neither free nor enslaved; he had no rights to exercise nor duties to fulfil. But on entering society, man contracted duties. Every such association being voluntary, the will alone of the associates could determine their reciprocal relationship; every such association existing through a pact, and being able to preserve itself only by establishing and enforcing laws, men were necessarily compelled, after uniting together, to impose upon themselves the duty of submitting to these laws and regarding them as circumscribing and determining their natural rights.

The Duc de Lévis also thought that the State should 'determine the rights and prescribe the duties of its members'. The Bishop of Langres, in defining the Constitution as 'a code and a body of law', was of the opinion that 'what was not law was a stranger to it'. Malouet warned the Assembly that the rights of man were to be found only in the Constitution, where they were fully developed and guaranteed. Mirabeau, speaking on August 17th, also emphasised the modifications which must limit in practice the natural rights of man. On the following day, Rhédon insisted that 'where there is no law there can be no society'. Biauzat emphasised the same point, as did the Comte d'Antraigues, whilst on the 30th Target suggested that 'whilst men lose their rights in uniting into civil society, they acquire much greater assurance of their confirmation'. De Landine claimed that, 'It is not with natural rights, fixed in the cradle of newly-born peoples, with which we are occupied, but with civil rights'.[1] Many more deputies held similar views. There can thus be no doubt that the Assembly did achieve, by implication, the subordination of individual rights to the over-riding power of the State.

Whether this was done of intention is a far less certain matter. There is at least an 'unverifiable probability' that fear of the masses led many of the members of the Right Wing and Centre parties to essay to limit too great an emphasis on individual right, in view of the lawless state of the country. What, however, leads us to suppose that the *étatiste* tendencies of the Declaration were the result rather of a largely unconscious evolution of ideas in the minds of the deputies was the somewhat vague use made by them of the phrase *la volonté générale*.

The origin of this phrase is uncertain. Montesquieu had used it as early as 1748 in the *Esprit des Lois*.[2] In 1755 it was used almost simultaneously by Diderot and Rousseau, the former in his

---

[1] Pellerin also insisted that a torch of freedom in the hands of peaceful men might well become an instrument of incendiarism in the hands of an *enragé*. (*Moniteur*, 1789, p. 176.)

[2] Livre XI, Chap. VI—'Les deux autres pouvoirs (exécutif et législatif) pourraient plutôt être donnés à des magistrats ou à des corps permanents, parce qu'ils ne s'exercent sur aucun particulier, n'étant l'un, que la volonté générale de l'Etat, et l'autre, que l'exécution de cette volonté générale.'

article on Natural Law and the latter in his Discourse on Political
Economy.   It was, of course, Rousseau who gave it its most detailed
development, particularly in the *Contrat Social*.   In the years which
followed the publication of this latter work, the term became popularised, as we have seen, by second and tenth rate writers, and by
pamphleteers to such an extent that not only had the term itself become
a *cliché*, but the concept of the sovereignty of the 'general will' had
become a leading tenet of the current *mystique*.   It was repeated *ad
nauseam* in the pamphlets which appeared during 1788 and 1789.   It
is to be found in many of the *cahiers* which reached Versailles.   From
1789 onwards it became a constant phrase on the lips of the Palais
Royal orators; it was repeated endlessly in the popular journals and in
the speeches of deputies in the Assembly itself.   It was constantly
heard in the Jacobin Club and in the branches later established by it
throughout the country.[1]

It is not possible to record the numerous occasions on which the
term was used in the Assembly.   During the debates on the Declaration of Rights it was on everybody's lips.   But the term continued to
have an equal currency during the following two years.   It was to be
used in most varied connections.   Thus Duport, for example, was to
claim that judges were 'officials charged with the maintenance of the
uniform execution of the law, that is, of the general will, common to
all the citizens of the empire'.   Liberty of the press was to be defended
as calculated to facilitate the determination of the 'general will' in large
communities, whilst the possession of private property was to be
justified as creating that sense of responsibility which would ensure the
stability of reasoning power, and so prevent the more extreme forms
of thought, often irresponsible, from unduly biasing the 'general will'.

But the term was never defined.   The Assembly never debated the
precise meaning which should attach to a phrase which it used continually.   A *cliché* it therefore remained, but it was a *cliché* which was to
prove of no small value during the following months, as we shall see.
It is, however, important at this stage to notice two important
advantages to the Assembly which arose from the current employment
of the term.

First of all, in carrying within itself, as it were, the idea of popular
sovereignty, the concept of the 'general will' precluded any resuscita-
tion of the idea of the divine right of the Bourbons.   'King by the
grace of God' had become 'King by the general will of the nation'.

[1] Cf. Brinton: *The Jacobins*, especially pp. 141 f.

The will of the people had been manifest on July 14th. Louis had accepted this will as decisive. But the Assembly had perceived the danger. This new power had to be treated with respect. A healthy fear of the mob which had no hesitation in threatening and even maltreating members of the Assembly itself was at least one reason why deputy after deputy preferred to identify his opinions and his resolutions with the supposed 'general will' of the nation.

But the concept of the 'general will' was valuable in another way. It epitomised, as it were, that *mystique* which had pervaded the masses, and which had become the driving force of the Revolution. But because it was national in scope, giving a new sense of dignity to the humblest citizen—and precisely because of this—it was a weapon which could be turned at will, not only against the privileged classes and the reactionaries, but against the Fourth Estate itself. To oppose it was to run the risk of being considered an enemy of the Revolution. Hence to formulate any policy, to lay down any rule in the Assembly, as being in accord with the 'general will' of the nation was often to spike the enemy's guns in advance. Resistance was possible only in terms of a right to question whether, in fact, this 'general will' had been correctly interpreted by one's opponent.

In identifying the sovereign power with the 'general will' of the people, therefore, the Declaration of Rights placed a potent weapon in the hands of the Assembly, or more particularly in the hands of the group which was to gain ascendancy in the Assembly. The implications of the extent of this power were not immediately obvious to the deputies. It was to grow in succeeding months, feeding upon the strains and stresses of a constitution-making task which was conditioned at all stages by these same twin fears of reaction in high places and the revolutionary ardour of the mob. The Declaration itself, in which were inherent the germs of *étatisme*, was a document in need of special interpretation. In succeeding chapters we shall examine the particular interpretation which was, in fact, to be given it by the National Assembly.

CHAPTER II

THE QUESTION OF THE VETO

WHATEVER may have been the final outcome of the measures decreed by the Assembly on the too famous night of August 4th, however limited were their effects to be after the subsequent process of legislation, there can be no doubt that the popular mind was greatly excited by the generally ill-informed and not infrequently misunderstood tidings of the concessions which had been made by the landowners and the feudal aristocracy. The Assembly's decision to strike a medal to commemorate the occasion, its command that a 'Te Deum' should be sung, and its determination that the King should be associated with this legislation as 'Restorer of French Liberty', gave the public every reason for optimism. Great, therefore, was the dismay and indignation when news reached Paris that Louis was unwilling to sanction either the decrees of August 4th or, indeed, the Declaration of Rights itself.

In the event, Louis had written to the Archbishop of Arles as early as August 5th stating that he would never sanction the decrees of the previous evening. The Assembly, however, had foreseen this possibility, and had determined, somewhat timidly, to assert itself as a truly constituent Assembly. For, as a constitution-making body, the deputies were prepared to insist that during the framing of the new constitution, all the powers of government as previously constituted, which included the King's legislative power, were in abeyance. Hence they had drafted the measures of August 4th as *arrêtés* instead of as *décrets*. The former merely required the King's consent for their publication, whilst the latter, in necessitating his sanction, would have implied a continuance of his legislative authority. Despite these precautions taken by the Assembly, the news of the King's opposition created such a stir in the capital and alarm amongst the deputies themselves that it was decided to deal immediately with the King's right, under the new Constitution, to veto legislation which had been enacted by the chosen representatives of the sovereign people.

Logically, there were many other matters which had first claim upon the attention of the Assembly. The size and structure of the legislature had not yet been determined, nor had the method of electing this body so much as been discussed. The position of the remaining powers of government, and their relationships to one another, had not been considered. Nevertheless, the problem of the veto appeared so fundamental that the Assembly agreed that it was not possible to postpone its settlement. And in view of the differences in the political outlook of the deputies which had become apparent during the later stages of the debate on the Declaration of Rights, it is not a matter for surprise that it was over the question of the veto that the first serious divergencies of opinion within the Assembly were to become apparent.

In point of fact, the controversy which arose in the Assembly was rather wider in scope than that of the veto alone. It was concerned with the entire position of the King as a participant in the legislative power. Was the King to participate in this power, and if so, in what manner?

Despite their acceptance of the doctrine of popular sovereignty, the Assembly had never opposed the preservation of the Monarchy as an institution. The *cahiers*, indeed, had unanimously demanded its retention; the popularity of the King at this time had been very great. They had also insisted upon his participation in the legislative power. The great majority of these documents recognised the necessity for the royal sanction to all acts of the legislative body. Within the Assembly, no single deputy openly advocated republican principles until after the King's flight to Varennes. Even after this incident, the majority of the deputies were to continue to insist upon the retention of the Monarchy as an integral part of the Constitution. There were many reasons for this.

Primarily, there was the fact that the Monarchy had existed for nearly one thousand years, and men tended almost instinctively to think in terms of a monarchical structure of government. Again, there was a national belief, so spontaneously evidenced in the *cahiers*, that the weaknesses hitherto associated with the Monarchy were due to the evil counsellors by whom the King had been surrounded. The nation thought in terms of the liberation of the King from his aristocratic advisers, from the corrupting influence of the Court. Freed from undue influence, the people at this time believed the King could do no wrong.

Further, there existed no precedent for the establishment of a republic in a country as large and as populous as France. There was a consciousness of the differences between a new country such as

America and an old country like France which had established traditions and a centuries-old historical development. Even Rousseau had
admitted the necessity for a monarchy in large states.[1]

Again, the deputies feared the effects of disrupting the Monarchy
on political grounds, for this may have resulted in a situation in which
the more extreme deputies of the Left, supported by the mob, may
have succeeded in carrying the Revolution beyond the point where the
majority of the deputies wished it to stop. The safeguarding of
the interests of the Third Estate appeared to them to necessitate the
wedding of the new political ideas to that stability in the State which
could be best ensured by a monarchical form of government.

As a *rentier* class, the wealthier members of the Third Estate also
tended to fear the effects of the dissolution of the Monarchy on purely
financial grounds, for the disturbances which would have followed
upon such a political upheaval would almost certainly have jeopardised
the security of every form of title to wealth.

And finally, there can be little doubt that the example of England,
a monarchy which was renowned throughout Europe as the home of
liberal ideas, fortified by the glowing accounts of Montesquieu and de
Lolme which idealised it as an example of a constitutional monarchy,
was not entirely without influence in French political circles.

Two possibilities lay open to the Assembly. Either the King could
be confined to the exercise of the executive power, or, in addition to
this, he could be allowed to participate in the legislative power. A
strict interpretation of the doctrine of the separation of the powers of
government, as also the implications of the principle of the sovereignty
of the 'general will' of the nation, appeared to favour the former
alternative. But so far as the separation of powers was concerned, it
could be argued that the principle was not violated by granting to the
King a limited right of participation in the affairs of the legislature, and
that such a right was indeed necessary to avoid the dangers of tyranny
which might arise were the legislative body to be subject to no will
outside its own.[2] And in so far as the sovereignty of the 'general will'
was concerned, was not some check upon the legislature necessary in
order to prevent the Assembly from misinterpreting the 'general will'
of the people?

Again, if the representative character of the legislature were to be
justified on the ground that it represented the 'general will' of the

[1] *Le Contrat Social*, Livre III, Chap. VI.
[2] Cf. Montesquieu: *L'Esprit des Lois*, Livre XI, Chap. VI.

nation,[1] then any fundamental difference in this respect between the bearers of the legislative power and the bearer of the executive power clearly broke down, for logically, if the legislative power could be transferred to a representative corporation, it could equally well be transferred to the King.   Both powers could then be regarded as equal, for both would derive their authority from a common source—the 'general will' of the sovereign people.

These, then, were the issues at the outset of the debates on the royal veto.   It should be pointed out, nevertheless, that a great majority of the deputies were anxious not only to carry out the instructions in their *cahiers* in this matter, which were summarised by one of their number as, 'Authority to regenerate the Monarchy, to reorganise the traditional régime on a sound basis; that is to say, to organise a State on a dual foundation, in which the sovereign appears in a two-fold capacity, the King and the People', but also to implement a monarchical form of government.   Without the veto, the government would have been virtually indistinguishable from that of a republic.

It was during the debates on the veto that the Assembly first divided up into a Right Wing, a Centre Party and a Left Wing.   By the end of October, largely because of its policy towards the veto, the extreme Right Wing was to be decimated, its members fleeing from the fury of the Paris mob.   Whilst certain of its more hardy members, such as Cazalès, remained, thereafter the constitutional decisions reached in the Assembly were the outcome of forceful, and often fiery, debate between a majority of the remaining deputies who formed the Left Centre, or Constitutional Party, and vociferous minorities composed of deputies attached to the Right Centre and to the extreme Left Wing respectively, who were generally in opposition.   The debate on the veto was the last debate in which the original strength of the extreme Right Wing Group in the Assembly was to be in action.

The extreme Right Wing and the Right Centre, or Monarchists, were in favour of the grant to the King of the absolute veto.   These deputies were principally concerned with practical considerations rather than theoretical arguments.   Mounier pointed out at the beginning of the debate that, 'In France, we are not deprived of all fundamental laws proper to the establishment of a constitution.   For fourteen hundred years we have had a King.   The sceptre has not been created by force, but by the will of the people . . . the King has always been appealed to by the people to right their wrongs, even when he was

[1] See Chapter III.

enchained by a feudal aristocracy.' Not only was the veto necessary to protect the interests of the people from the possible tyranny of future Assemblies, but in order that the head of the executive power might be able to defend himself, since 'all bodies have a tendency to add to their power, and the Assembly might tend to encroach upon the executive power, which latter would be at their mercy without the defensive arm of the veto'. Finally, in Mounier's view, the prestige of the King necessitated his participation in the legislative power. De Lameth reinforced these arguments on the following day.

Deschamps expressed himself more strongly. 'When we were sent to the Estates General,' he pointed out, 'we were not told to make a new Constitution, but to regenerate an old one; we were not told to erect our government within the framework of a monarchy, but to re-confirm our ancient Monarchy. You cannot deliberate on the royal sanction, for we have one.' Virieu and Lally-Tollendal were equally insistent upon this point of view.

The two strongest speeches, however, in favour of the absolute veto were made by Mirabeau and the Comte d'Antraigues. In the course of a long address Mirabeau claimed that the greater the nation, the more important did it become that a single and supreme chief should be capable of dealing with those internal convulsions inevitable in a large country, and be vested with sufficient power to reunite all parties and turn their activities towards a common centre. Called by his high office to be at once the executor of the law and the protector of his people, 'the Monarch might be forced to unite his people against the government were he not given the right to ensure, by his power of sanctioning the laws, that all legislation was in accordance with the general will of the people'.

Mirabeau was against a suspensive veto. He claimed that there was no guarantee that a subsequent legislature would be any nearer a true interpretation of the 'general will' than had been the first. Further, it was most unlikely that any King would be tempted to prolong his veto in opposition to the known wishes of his people. 'When the law is safeguarded by public opinion,' he declared, 'it becomes absolutely imperative that the royal power shall be used to protect and defend it. At what moment may one count most on the empire of public opinion? Is it not when the head of the executive has himself given his consent to the law, and when knowledge of his consent has reached all citizens?'

Mirabeau finally showed that he anticipated a refusal of the royal

D

sanction in two cases only—where the King judged that a proposed law would not further the interests of the nation, and where, deceived by his ministers, he resisted a law contrary to its expressed views.   In such a case, deprived of the veto, would not the King and his ministers take illegal or violent means to avoid such legislation?   On the other hand, given the use of the veto, would not its employment under the eyes of the entire nation prevent recourse to such illegal, violent or underhand methods?

How could the veto injure the sovereignty of the people, it was argued, when 'it is no more than a right which is vested by the people in the King, who has an equal interest in preventing the growth of a too powerful aristocracy'.   Without the veto, the representative body would itself become a veritable aristocracy against which the people would have no remedy except 'through a natural and inevitable alliance with the King'.

Whilst Mirabeau insisted upon the grant of an absolute veto to the King on realistic grounds, the Comte d'Antraigues followed Montesquieu's argument.[1]   He concluded that whilst a complete separation of the powers of government was essential for the preservation of liberty, that very liberty might disappear if a check on the power of the legislature were not provided by the King's right to veto legislation. 'In monarchical states', he asserted, 'two risks have to be run—the reunion of powers in the legislature, which constitutes the tyranny of several, and the reunion of powers in the executive, which constitutes the tyranny of one.   To preserve liberty between two such dangerous extremes, it is necessary to oppose one against the other. . . .   In the royal sanction, the people find the rampart of public liberty, and the assurance, that we, who are its representatives, shall never become its masters.'

These arguments were supported by de Sèze, the Abbé Maury and de Custine.   Malouet, in particular, insisted that the deputies had private wills which would not truly reflect, but might betray, the 'general will' of the nation.   Only the King was above private interest.

Malouet, however, found himself aligned with those deputies who favoured the grant of a suspensive veto to the King.   Only in this way, in his opinion, could the veto be reconciled with the principle of the sovereignty of the 'general will' of the nation.   It was possible that the representative body might misinterpret this 'general will'.   A

[1] Cf. *L'Esprit des Lois*, Livre XI, Chap. VI.

means must be provided by which the people itself could correct this error. But the veto once applied, 'if the people persisted in their demand for the enactment of a law, and again charged their representatives to press for it, the King had neither the right nor the means to resist'. Both King and legislature must bow before the declared will of the nation. 'The ultimate judge', declared de Lameth, 'is the nation. It is the nation alone which is ultimately responsible for its own well being. The King might oppose the Assembly, but never the general will of the people.'

The party of the Left Centre, composed of the more moderate elements in the Assembly, and known as the Constitutionalists from October onwards, was generally in favour of the suspensive veto. Fearing the King, it was determined to support, and legislate in terms of, the essential principle of the sovereignty of the 'general will'. But it recognised the monarchical character of the State. To refuse a right of veto was to play into the hands of the extreme Left Wing, who were more and more inclined to identify themselves with the more advanced democratic principles of the Paris mobs, for whom the Constitutionalists had an equally healthy respect.

Hence the majority of the deputies, who identified themselves with the Left Centre, favoured a suspensive veto. It was 'an appeal to the nation by the King, upon which the people alone, in whom all power resided, could judge', said Pétion de Villeneuve. And as Beaumetz added, 'Why have greater confidence in a delegate succeeding by chance than in delegates freely elected by their fellow-citizens?'

Rabaut de St. Etienne was concerned with the awkward position in which an absolute right of veto might place the King. 'Nothing could be more unfortunate for the King', he claimed, 'than to expose him to the misfortune of being able to oppose the laws which might be demanded by his people'. But Mounier took a different view of this. He insisted that to make the people the judge of a conflict between the King and the Assembly would be to elevate it above the constituted powers. Then, the nation, 'flattered by the increase of power in the hands of those whom it had chosen, would always support the Assembly; it would be misled into always opposing the King in the name of liberty; the deputies newly elected after the veto had been used would consider themselves bound by a mandate, despite the abolition by the Constitution of the imposition of any mandate on a representative of the nation'.

On the other hand, the extreme Left Wing were against any veto

at all.   The opposition was led by Sieyès, who argued that as the law
was essentially the will of the governed, the governors could have no
part in its formation.   The position of the King could be looked at
from three points of view.   He could be looked upon as a citizen, as a
king, or as head of the executive power.   As a citizen, his influence
was no greater than that of any other citizen—it was confined to that
of his individual will.   As a king, he presided over the government
and pronounced the laws made by the nation through its chosen
representatives.   As head of the executive power, he was no more than
an agent, and his functions were limited to those entrusted to him to
ensure the efficient execution of the law.

'It is vain', exclaimed Sieyès, 'to say that the King should influence
the making of the law.   If his will is capable of being equivalent to
that of two constituted powers of government, it is capable of equalling
that of twenty-five million people. . . .   If it were, it would mean that
the will of an individual would triumph over the general will.   The
formation of the law is the result of individual wills coalescing, one
with another.   If the King can impede this process, his particular will
can impose itself on the general will, which cannot and should not be.'

Sieyès concluded by defining the royal veto as a *lettre de cachet*
launched against the 'general will'.   In his conclusion he was supported by de Crenières, de Crillon and de Polverel, amongst other
deputies.

De Landine opposed the veto for rather different reasons.   'Whether
the veto be suspensive or absolute', he asserted, 'I believe it to be none
the less dangerous.   If it be absolute, it will confound the legislative
power.   If it be suspensive, it will foster quarrels and perpetuate
factions.'

By the middle of September, however, it was clear that the greater
number of deputies favoured the middle course of a suspensive veto
which, whilst preserving the monarchical principle, did not impair the
concept of the sovereignty of the 'general will' of the nation.   But,
granted the suspensive veto, within what limits was it to operate?   Four
main lines of thought emerged during the discussions on this problem.

Primarily, many deputies, including de la Rochefoucauld, de Castellane and Rabaut de St. Etienne, favoured the suggestion that the King
should yield when a second legislature had confirmed the views of
the first.   They based their opinion upon the ground that the nation
having been consulted, the 'general will' of the people had been
ascertained.

A second point of view was put forward by Goupil de Préfeln, amongst other deputies, who advocated that the King should be compelled to yield if a three-quarters majority were obtained in favour of the disputed piece of legislation in each of two successive legislatures. Thirdly, de Lameth, who was worried by the effect of possible delay, suggested that after an act of the legislature had been vetoed by the King, an immediate appeal to the nation should be made in order that the 'general will' should be ascertained at the earliest possible moment. Finally, Thouret suggested that the veto should extend over two successive legislatures, but become inoperative in the third.

There was considerable discussion over the rival merits of these divergent proposals. It was argued that if the King had to yield to a second legislature, his veto would be ineffective, and this would deter him from exercising it at all. On the other hand, where it extended to a third legislature there could be no doubt that the King would be yielding, not to the Assembly, but to the clearly expressed will of the nation. Thus, as de Sèze pointed out, not only would his dignity be preserved, but he would be given time to discover the true 'general will' of the people.

The fourth alternative gained the day and, on September 15th, the Assembly adopted the suspensive veto by 673 votes to 325 votes. The leading characteristic of the debates was undoubtedly the way in which each political group had striven to identify its policy with the necessity for securing a true interpretation of the 'general will'. The Right Wing had supported the absolute veto as an instrument necessary to prevent the King's taking more violent steps to stop legislation which he did not consider in conformity with the 'general will' of the nation. The Left Centre advocated a suspensive veto for similar reasons, but objected to the absolute veto on the grounds that it itself violated the principle of the sovereignty of the 'general will'. Finally, the Left Wing opposed the veto as being a *lettre de cachet* launched against the 'general will' of the people.

In the meantime, the 'general will' of the Paris mob was being made known in no uncertain fashion. The debates in the Assembly had been accompanied by increasing agitation on the part of the sovereign people. In the alleys of the Palais Royal, the Paris mansion of the Duc d'Orléans, which he had placed at the disposal of revolutionary orators with some hope of securing popular support for his designs on the throne, more and more violent attacks were made upon those members of the Assembly who had supported the veto. It is probable that the mass of the people had little idea of what the veto implied. 'Do you know what the veto means?' cried the agitators. 'Listen, then! You go home, where your wife has prepared your dinner. The King says "Veto".—No dinner!' As for the suspensive veto itself, whilst some people vaguely believed that it was concerned with the King's unrestricted right to 'suspend', or hang, his opponents, others seem to have regarded it as a human being. 'What is he this Veto? What has he done, this brigand Veto?'

In particular, it was generally believed that the grant of the veto to the King would lead directly to a rescission of the *arrêtés* of August 4th, and, in consequence, more than forty members of the Assembly received letters threatening their lives were they to continue to support it. Several, including Lally-Tollendal, were attacked in the street. One letter, perhaps, may be quoted. It was that sent to the President of the Assembly himself.

'The Patriotic Assembly of the Palais Royal', so ran this document, 'have the honour to inform you that if a portion of the aristocracy, composed of a party in the Clergy, a party in the Nobility, and 120 members of the Commons, ignorant and corrupt, continue to disturb the peace by demanding the absolute veto, 15,000 men are ready to light up their houses and châteaux, and yours in particular, Monsieur, and to inflict on these deputies who betray their country the fate of Foulon and Berthier'.[1]

In view of such pressure, it was becoming increasingly plain to the Assembly that if its authority were to be preserved, and the wider interests of the Third Estate safeguarded, measures must be taken to neutralise this growing power of the masses in the Constitution which they were endeavouring to formulate. How could such measures be introduced without violating the tenets of the current *mystique* or modifying the doctrine of the sovereign power of the 'general will' of the people? Much of the legislation which followed the enacting of the suspensive veto was to be indirectly designed to this end. But two problems which were to tax the ingenuity of the Assembly called for immediate solution. The first was how to define the powers of the Assembly in such a way as to remove them from a theoretical dependence upon the 'general will' of the nation, a concept upon which the orators of the Palais Royal were laying so much stress—and this without violating the principles which had been embodied in the Declaration of Rights. The second was how to regulate the system of

[1] Bailly, op. cit., Vol. III, p. 392.

election to the legislature in such a way that there would be little danger of deputies reaching the Assembly whose sympathies might not be such as to ensure the preservation of that political system which the Third Estate regarded as both justifiable and valid.

CHAPTER III

THE REPRESENTATION OF THE SOVEREIGN PEOPLE

ARTICLE THREE of the Declaration of the Rights of Man and of the Citizen declared, *Le principe de toute souveraineté réside essentiellement dans la Nation. Nul corps, nul individu ne peut exercer d'autorité qui n'en émane expressément.* Article Six followed this up by asserting, *La loi est l'expression de la volonté générale. Tous les citoyens ont le droit de concourir personnellement ou par leurs représentants à sa formation.*

The sovereign people, as we have seen, was not unaware of its rights. It had demonstrated its power on more than one occasion. The Assembly, therefore, was faced with the unenviable task of translating these two abstract concepts into workable form in such a way that it retained real authority whilst pandering to the views of the mob, whose representatives were continuous spectators of its proceedings. To achieve this purpose, it was necessary for the deputies to regularise the authority of the Assembly in terms of the Declaration of Rights, and hence in terms of the current *mystique*, whilst at the same time ensuring that the 'general will' of the nation could not at any time rear its head in opposition to the will of the Assembly itself.

The issue was not a simple one. For whilst it was generally recognised that the Assembly was a body representative of the entire nation, what was not clear was the extent of the power which had been thus delegated by the sovereign people. Were the deputies, in effect, to be regarded as *commettants*, that is, as representatives who were entitled to use their own judgment and formulate their own decisions in the Assembly—as representatives, that is, who were for a period of time to regard themselves as cloaked with the ultimate authority of their constituents—or were they no more than *mandataires*, men who were merely mouthpieces of their electors, bound hand and foot by the *cahier* with which each one of them had been furnished and subject at all times to the will of their electors?

First of all, it was necessary to establish the content of the 'general will'. Theoretically, such a will could only be made manifest in an assembly of the whole nation, but, as Mounier pointed out on September 4th, 1789, even this form of direct democracy had not prevented certain of the Greek Republics from allowing themselves to be seduced into accepting the reign of tyrants.[1] From the beginning, however, the deputies had recognised the impossibility of such a meeting in a country the size of France. De Crénières, after carefully defining *la volonté générale* as the 'will of the greatest number', which was 'the will of all', showed that 'Frenchmen, considering that it was impossible for them all to assemble in one place, and there to communicate to each other their intentions, and so formulate the general will, have assembled together in different places, and have fully chosen in each province, or in each part of a province, deputies whom they have sent to Versailles to constitute them into a free people'. This statement met with general approval, but there resulted a cleavage of opinion in the Assembly as to the extent to which it was in a position to interpret the will of the sovereign people.

Several deputies insisted that they were no more than *mandataires* and that they were consequently bound by an imperative mandate. They asserted that the 'general will' of the nation could not be ascertained, much less enforced, unless every section of the nation were represented by deputies each of whom pronounced only the will of his electors and was continually subject to the control of his constituents. On June 26th, both Lally-Tollendal and Clermont-Tonnerre indicated that they did not intend to exceed in any way the instructions which had been laid down for them in their *cahiers*, without referring back to their constituents for further guidance.

Pétion de Villeneuve was another strong supporter of the imperative mandate. 'The members of the legislative body are *mandataires*', he declared. 'The citizens who have chosen them are *commettants*; hence, these representatives are subjected to the will of those from whom they derive their powers'. He was, however, less dogmatic in his interpretation of the mandatory system than were the two previously mentioned deputies; he was, for instance, prepared to allow the deputies the use of their discretion in deciding matters upon which they had received no explicit guidance. 'It is necessary that there should be a sanction, but to what extent should it be operative?' he asked. 'If

---

[1] It may be noted that both Montesquieu, in his description of these Republics, as also Rousseau, in *Le Contrat Social*, had denied that the 'general will' of the nation could be ascertained through representatives. (Livre II, Chap. III, and Livre III, Chap. XII).

our constituents have alone prescribed such a sanction, we are masters
of the latitude which it permits. We find ourselves obliged to interpret this sanction, for since the degree of influence to be permitted was
not laid down in our *cahiers*, the sanction may be determined by each
of us.'

In point of fact, the imperative mandate was not unknown in
France. From the beginning of the sixteenth century, deputies to the
Estates General had been commonly bound by the instructions contained in their *cahiers*. But there was one fundamental difference
between this procedure and that which theoretically would have
resulted in a reproduction of the 'general will' of the nation. In the
Estates General, each deputy had only the special interests of his own
particular constituents to consider. There had been no thought of
his pretending to interpret the 'general will' of the people as a whole.

Nevertheless, other deputies, including Rabaut de St. Etienne and
Duport, were equally insistent upon their duty to interpret their
mandates rigidly, whilst Rhédon was even more emphatic. 'We are
not the nation', he asserted. 'What rights have we? None! What
duties are we obliged to fulfil? The rights of our constituents, which
we have to exercise.'

The Assembly was embarrassed. In view of their declaration
concerning the 'general will', such arguments appeared reasonable.
But at the same time the deputies were becoming increasingly aware
of the danger of legislating on such a basis, with the inevitable prospect
of continual outside interference with their work, and with the work
of subsequent Assemblies.

An alternative scheme was suggested by de Crenières, who advocated the preservation of the initiative of the citizen by recognising his
right to promote legislation and, where necessary, amend existing laws.
This alternative was in turn taken up by Rabaut, who claimed that
where the people were too numerous to assemble, they should be
empowered to commission deputies for the express purpose of making
known their will. He insisted that the people could never surrender
their right to participate in the legislative power without losing their
sovereignty. The scheme, however, suffered from the same defects
as the imperative mandate itself.

It was Sieyès who first saw a method of avoiding the difficulty.
Primarily, he pointed out that the adoption of the imperative mandate
could not be regarded as a satisfactory substitute for the general meeting
of all the citizens in the State. For though in theory it was each

deputy's duty to interpret the 'general will' of the people as a whole, in essence, where each deputy took his mandate seriously, he was in little better case than had been the deputies of earlier Estates Generals, for he represented a particular set of interests, and the more strictly he interpreted his mandate, the more limited became his power to interpret the wider interests of the nation.

'A deputy', he insisted, 'is nominated by one bailliage in the name of all bailliages; a deputy is thus nominated by the entire nation. All citizens are his electors. For in the assembly of a bailliage, you would not wish that a deputy who has just been elected should charge himself with the will of a small number against the will of the majority; you would not desire that a deputy of all the citizens of the kingdom should listen alone to the wishes of the inhabitants of a bailliage or of a municipality against the wishes of the entire nation. I believe', he concluded, 'that no bailliage has the right to give an imperative order to its representative. The will of a bailliage is no more than an individual will. All individual wills must be subordinated to the general will. No representative should be bound by his *cahier*. He should be able to modify the will of his electors according to the will of the State. He is an immediate deputy of his bailliage, but a mediate deputy of the nation.'

Sieyès' great contribution, however, was his suggested distinction between the substance and the exercise of political power. The substance of power undoubtedly resided in the 'general will' of the mass of the people, but the people, he claimed, could be regarded as having delegated the exercise of this power to their representatives. Within the Assembly, the deputies would determine a 'representative general will'. Sieyès was particularly emphatic about the recognition of this principle. 'The great majority of our fellow-citizens have neither the knowledge nor the leisure to wish to concern themselves directly with the government of France.'

His proposals were taken up with enthusiasm by all but the more extreme deputies of the Left Centre. Talleyrand, Roederer, Mounier and Malouet, in a series of speeches between August 8th and 12th all developed this idea. Opposition, however, came from several deputies who still favoured a closer approach to the spirit of direct democracy. Salles was the most insistent of these deputies. He persisted in demanding a more direct exercise of the sovereign power by the mass of the people. In particular, he claimed that were a difference of opinion to arise between the Assembly and the King, it was the duty

of the King to explain to the primary assemblies the reason for his
veto and the people should then directly express its will in this matter.
Pétion also strongly supported this viewpoint.

After Sieyès had met this argument by pointing out that in fact the
powers delegated to the Assembly were, in reality, essentially subordinate, and that the *volonté commune représentative* was but a reflection of *la grande volonté commune*, (a point which was taken up by
Barère, who showed that 'The mandatory authority does not hand
over to its delegates the powers possessed by itself.   It is not a legislative body.   The legislative power is operative only from the moment
when the representatives first meet together as a representative
assembly'), the Assembly passed on to decree that whilst the sovereign
power belonged to the nation, from which all powers emanated, the
Constitution was representative, the representatives being the legislative
body and the King.

As a reply to further criticism from the Left Wing that such a
separation of the substance from the exercise of the sovereign power
was merely a polite fiction, and that the substance of power divorced
from its exercise had no reality, Mounier and Robespierre, amongst
other deputies, pointed out that the supremacy of the people was secure
in that they perpetually exercised a censorship over the acts of the
Assembly.   The people could, at any time, deprive the Assembly of
its authority by exercising its right to modify the Constitution of the
country, for the constituent power could reside nowhere but in the
'general will' of the nation.   Robespierre was particularly emphatic on
this point.   Were the people deprived of such a right, he considered
that the State would cease to exist.

In this way, the Assembly believed that it had largely overcome the
difficulties presented by its adoption of the representative principle.   It
had perpetuated the fiction of the 'general will' by investing it with the
'substance' of the sovereign power and, by retaining the exercise of this
power, had largely succeeded in protecting itself from external interference without violating a leading tenet of the current *mystique*.   It
had also avoided arousing the political suspicions of the masses.

The matter was to be raised again in 1791 during the debate on the
re-eligibility of deputies for election to the Legislative Assembly.
Despite the deterioration in the relationship between the people and
the Assembly which had set in by this time, exactly the same arguments
were used.   Thus, on May 16th, Thouret said, 'The fundamental
basis of representative government is the right of election; this right

is the only one exercised by the people itself.' On August 10th Roederer claimed that 'the essence of representation is that each individual represented lives and deliberates through his representative and has, by means of a free election, identified his will with the will of his representative', whilst Barnave asserted that constitutional representation consisted in 'willing' on behalf of the nation.

Thus the sovereignty of the people was, in fact, transformed into a *droit d'élire*, if we except, and reserve for later discussion, the shadowy authority bound up with its theoretical retention of the constituent power. The Assembly had not been divided on the issue, if we exclude a certain measure of criticism from members of the Left Wing, which we have examined in some detail above. The next step which it was to take, however, was to receive a much stormier reception, both from the Left Wing in the Assembly and from the mob outside. This step was a proposal to limit the franchise to 'active citizens' alone.

Such a step appeared to be the more necessary because of the events of October 5th. In compelling the royal family to take up residence in Paris, whence they had been followed by an unwilling Assembly, the mob had again successfully followed the line of direct action. Again the Assembly had been forced to accede grudgingly to the *fait accompli* of the sovereign people. At first in the *Archevêché*, and later in the *Manège*, with the executive power close at hand in the Tuileries, and the Palais Royal nearby, the deputies found their activities more closely supervised than they had been at Versailles. So many of the members of the Right Wing, alarmed by the threats of the mob and increasingly conscious that their influence was waning, asked for their passports, that difficulties had to be placed in the way of their receiving them. Nevertheless, more than three hundred deputies present at Versailles failed to turn up in Paris. As a result the Assembly gained in political homogeneity, but almost certainly suffered from a withdrawal of many first-rate political thinkers.

The removal of the Assembly to Paris had not only established it in the midst of the sovereign people. It had enabled reports of the debates to be more easily circulated and more promptly criticised in the flood of newspapers which had sprung up after the removal of the censorship. The more important ones such as Brissot's *Le Patriote Français*, Barère's *Le Point du Jour*, Mallet du Pan's *Mercure*, Prudhomme's weekly *Les Révolutions de Paris* and later Pancoucke's *Le Moniteur*, attained national stature. Not only were many of the deputies to become more and more prone to voice their particular views in such papers, especially when they had failed to obtain a hearing in the Assembly, but the pillorying of any particular deputy in such papers not infrequently placed his very life in danger. Deputies who had voted for the absolute veto knew they were marked men. Thibaudeau, for example, slept with his bedroom door bolted, guarded by his son, who, armed with pistol and sword, occupied the anteroom. Necker frequently woke from sleep in a cold sweat at the thought of what might happen were the bread supply in Paris to fail for twenty-four hours. Bailly, referring to the Palais Royal, said he could rest tranquil only on rainy days.

A further result of the Assembly's establishment in the capital was the growth and development of the political clubs. The Breton Club had been founded at Versailles by the deputies from Brittany as a meeting-place where the problems of the day could be discussed outside the walls of the *Salle des Menus Plaisirs*.[1]   In Paris, the Club, newly styled the *Société des Amis de la Constitution*, took over premises which had been previously occupied by the Dominican monks in the Rue St. Honoré, nicknamed the Jacobins. The Club was subsequently known by this name. There, its membership speedily increased, its politics becoming roughly identified with those of the Constitutional Group in the Assembly.   Only after the flight of the King to Varennes was the Jacobin Club, which then identified itself with the growing republican outlook of Paris, to move away from the policy of the Left Centre, and to lose the adherence of the more moderate deputies, who separated from it to found the rival club of the *Feuillants*.

The club of the 'opposition', if it is permissible to give it this title, was the *Société des Amis des Droits de l'Homme et du Citoyen*.   It took its nickname, the 'Cordeliers', from the name of the street in which its headquarters, the Franciscan Monastery, was situated.   Its politics were those of the Left Wing in the Assembly.[2]   More radical than the Jacobins, it tended to reflect the interests of the *petite bourgeoisie*. It was of lower social status, and as its name implied, it stood for a more rigid interpretation of the Declaration of Rights in the Constitution itself.

Other clubs, set up mainly to counteract the influence of the Jacobins and the Cordeliers, ranged from the ultra-royalist *Amis du Roi*,

[1] Bouchard, A.: *Le Club Breton*, pp. 38 f.

[2] Mathiez, A.: *Le Club des Cordeliers*, p. 23.—'Au début de leur existence, les Cordeliers n'avaient pas d'autre politique que de faire la guerre aux aristocrates, d'autre doctrine que celle des chefs du côté gauche à l'Assemblée Constituante, dont ils suivaient d'ordinaire les directions.'

the conservative *Impartiaux* frequented by Malouet, Lafayette's *Club du '89* and Lally-Tollendal's *Club Monarchique*, to the *Cercle Social* which was mildly socialist and republican in character.

The proximity of the Jacobins and the Cordeliers to the *Manège*, on the northern side of the Tuileries gardens, to which the Assembly had moved after a three weeks' stay in the *Archevêché*, increased the popularity of the evening meetings in the clubs,[1] where the proceedings of the day in the Assembly were discussed, not infrequently before a large audience. As the months went by, the debates in the clubs, particularly in the Jacobins, became almost of as great importance as those in the Assembly itself, and matters to be introduced in the Assembly were not infrequently debated during the previous evening in the Club. The leaders of the Assembly regularly attended and joined in the debates.[2]

A great increase in the number of provincial clubs affiliated to the Jacobin Club in Paris took place from 1789 onwards. Brinton estimates that some 6,800 such clubs had secured affiliation by the end of 1789, with an estimated membership of one million subscribers.[3] By means of an extended system of correspondence, almost all centres of political influence in the country were kept in touch with affairs in the capital. What Paris thought thereby became a potential factor in the political outlook of the country.

Paris was rapidly becoming a 'microcosm' of the sovereign people for another reason. After the night of August 4th, the peasantry had largely lost interest in political events. They had gained more than they had hitherto dreamed of in their most optimistic moments. On the other hand, the larger provincial cities, such as Lyons, Bordeaux, Rheims, Marseilles and Rennes, were not big enough for members of the Fourth Estate to exercise any form of political pressure. Apart from their relatively small populations, and the rigidity of the social structure which still characterised them, they were too isolated from one another for artisans and workers to make common cause.

Hence it was in Paris, and in Paris alone, that the conditions existed for the possible success of any popular movement opposed to the political views of the Third Estate, as represented by the majority group in the Assembly. Established in the capital, therefore, the

---

[1] Cf. Bouchard, A.: op. cit., p. 86. The famous night of August 4th was preceded by a debate on feudalism on August 3rd in the Club.

[2] Aulard: *Société des Jacobins*, Vol. III, pp. 335, 345.

[3] Op. cit., p. 42.

deputies were compelled to proceed warily in putting forward their new electoral system. They had to take the greatest care to ensure that their proposals were reconcilable with the principle of the sovereignty of the 'general will'. For the King was becoming more and more unpopular with the masses. The events which had preceded the march on Versailles—the delay in the King's ratification of the decrees of August 4th and the Declaration of Rights, the insults to the tricolour and the attempts to suborn the National Guard—had appeared to the mob to be irreconcilable with the decision of the Assembly to grant the veto to the King. The suspicion that the Assembly was too favourably inclined towards the Monarchy and the aristocracy had been further reinforced by the volume of support in favour of the establishment of a Second Chamber. Hence every step in the decline of the popularity of the King tended to reflect a corresponding decline in the prestige of the Assembly. Paris was rapidly becoming more democratic than its government.

It therefore appeared necessary to the majority of deputies that steps must be taken to ensure that in the next and subsequent Assemblies, the representation should reflect a political outlook which was of a sufficiently bourgeois character to ensure that the necessary reforms which the Third Estate deemed valid having been secured, the Revolution should stop. It was therefore necessary to exclude from power more radically minded deputies, who, popularly elected by the masses, might sabotage the framework which was in process of erection. Thus far had the Left Centre, under the pressure of events, and with the support of the Right Wing, moved away from the principles of the Declaration of Rights.

The method adopted by the Assembly was to institute a distinction between active and passive citizenship. By limiting the franchise to members of a propertied class, the deputies believed that they could ensure the retention of political power by the Third Estate, and so preserve the Constitution from attack by the more radically inclined masses. 'All the inhabitants of a country', Sieyès claimed, 'should enjoy the rights of passive citizenship; all have the right to protection of their person, their liberty and their property. . . . But all have not the right to play an active part in the formation of the public powers; all are not active citizens. The women at least, the children, the foreigners, and they who contribute nothing to sustain the public establishment, should not directly influence public affairs. All may enjoy the advantage of society, but they alone who contribute to the public establishment are the true shareholders in the great public enterprise. They alone are truly the active citizens, and true members of the association.'

This linking of active citizenship with property ownership, the right to vote with taxable capacity, was all very well. But what of the sovereignty of the 'general will'? How was such a policy to be reconciled with Article III of the Declaration of Rights, which stated, *Le principe de toute souveraineté réside essentiellement dans la nation; nul corps, nul individu ne peut exercer d'autorité qui n'en émane expressément?*

It was Barnave who found a way out of this difficulty. He claimed that both the electors and the elected acted by virtue of an office entrusted to them by the 'general will' of the nation as a whole. The duties of an elector and his right to vote were not the exercise of a civil right but the exercise of a commission, a commission which was not granted by any one district but by the whole of the nation. 'All who have disagreed with the Committee', he declared, 'have made a fundamental mistake. They have confounded the rights of the people with the quality of elector which society determines with a view to its well-comprehended interests . . . the function of being an elector is not a right; I repeat that it exists for society, which has a right to determine its conditions. Representative government has but one snare to fear—that of corruption. In order that it should be essentially sound, it is necessary to guarantee the purity and incorruptibility of the electoral body, which should, therefore, be protected by three fundamental guarantees: the first, knowledge, and it cannot be denied that the possession of a certain amount of wealth is the most certain measure of a better education and a more extended knowledge; the second, an interest in affairs . . . and the third, independence of fortune, which places the elector above corruption.'

Barnave's point was that opponents of active citizenship were confusing a democratic with a representative constitution, and the rights of man with the quality of elector. This latter he conceived to be a public function to which no one had a right, but which was regulated by society in its own interests. Only in a truly democratic system could such an electoral function be considered a right of man; in a representative system it most certainly was not a right. Barère supported this argument, as did Thouret, who said, 'The function of an elector is founded on a public commission, whose powers must be determined by the nation itself.' Many other deputies also favoured this viewpoint.

It is interesting to note that both Rousseau[1] and Mably,[2] in the model constitutions which they respectively drew up for Poland, had visualised a limitation of the suffrage on the grounds of capacity. *Affranchir les peuples de Pologne est une grande et belle opération*, wrote Rousseau, *mais hardie, périlleuse, et qu'il ne faut pas tenter inconsidérément* . . . *N'affranchissez leurs corps qu'après avoir affranchi leurs âmes. Sans ce préliminaire, comptez que votre opération réuissira mal.* And equally Mably. *Il est naturel qu'un possesseur de fonds prenne plus d'intérêt à la chose publique que celui qui ne possède rien en propre. D'ailleurs, un homme qui est soumis aux ordres d'un maître est indigne de porter un suffrage quand il faut décider des lois d'un peuple libre.*

The Constitutional Committee's proposed qualifications for active citizenship were French nationality, the attainment of an age of twenty-five years, residence for at least one year in a canton, liability for the payment of a direct tax annually of at least the value of three days' work as determined by the appropriate provincial assembly, and finally proof of 'non-servile status', which was defined as a personal relationship not incompatible with that independence which was a necessary adjunct of the free exercise of political rights.[3]

The Committee announced that the representative system of the country should have a triple basis of territory, population and taxable capacity, and so far as taxable capacity was concerned, they proposed that the districts contributing most to the expenses of the State should have a proportionately larger representation.

Thouret explained that his committee had been concerned to establish a just proportion between the primary assemblies, which would consist of the active members of each canton, and the departmental committees, consisting of the deputies elected by these primary assemblies. 'The number of individuals in France', he stated, 'is about twenty-six millions, but after reasonably accurate calculations, the number of active citizens, after deducting women, minors and all those who for other legitimate reasons are deprived of the exercise of political rights, is reduced to one-sixth of the total population. Only approximately four million four hundred thousand citizens have, there-

---

[1] Considérations sur le gouvernement de Pologne.

[2] Du gouvernement et des lois de Pologne.

[3] The Committee was careful to point out that the servile status referred to was not to include 'des anciens mains mortables dont la servitude a d'ailleurs été abolie par le décret de l'Assemblée Nationale du 4 août'. They referred rather to a citizen 'dans l'état de domesticité, c'est-à-dire, un serviteur à gages'. Clearly, such a definition was capable of a wide interpretation.

fore, been counted as eligible to vote in the primary assemblies of their cantons'.

'But', continued Thouret, 'equality of tenure is specious and false if it is not modified by the balance of indirect taxes which serve to re-establish the equilibrium of values, and it is because of this that the basis of taxation is doubtless of secondary importance when it is a question of balancing political rights as between one individual and another, without which personal equality would be destroyed and the aristocracy of riches established; but this inconvenience disappears entirely when the incidence of taxation is considered only in the aggregate, and only as between province and province. It then serves to apportion justly the reciprocal rights of the cities, without compromising the personal rights of the citizen. Thus', he concluded, 'the committee feels that so far as the primary assembly is concerned, itself a fundamental element in the system of representation, regard should be had only to population. Each man, provided that he is an active citizen, must be enabled to enjoy his individual rights by the performance of this primary duty.'

The remainder of Thouret's speech was devoted to explaining the mechanism of the proposed system. From each primary assembly, one deputy was to be elected for every two hundred electors, which meant that the active citizens between them would elect twenty-two thousand deputies to seven hundred and twenty communal assemblies. But a further qualification for election to the assembly of the commune was the payment by each such deputy of an annual tax equivalent to the value of ten days' work as provincially assessed.

At this stage, proportional representation was to be secured as follows. Two hundred and forty deputies were to be elected on a territorial basis, three from each of the eighty departments. Secondly, one deputy was to be elected for every two hundred and forty active citizens resident in each department. And thirdly, the total amount of direct taxes payable in the kingdom having been divided into two hundred and forty parts, one deputy was to be elected for each two hundred and fortieth part of this total paid in each department.

Thus seven hundred and sixty deputies were to reach the National Assembly. A final qualification for their eligibility was, however, proposed. This was the annual payment by any such elected deputy of a direct tax of at least one *marc d'argent*, equivalent roughly to fifty days' wages.

The Left Wing had become more and more infuriated as the

electoral plan of the Constitutionalists was unfolded. It confirmed their fears that the wealthier bourgeoisie were directing the revolution away from the earlier ideals which it had embodied. More and more it became apparent that the people were to be sovereign in name alone. The end of Thouret's speech, therefore, was the signal for a violent attack by the more radical deputies. They were led by Robespierre, who, jealous of the right of the small property owner now virtually excluded from representation, made a heated attack upon the plan. He insisted that it was contrary to the spirit of the Declaration of Rights. 'All men are equal in rights', he declared, 'and every man is a citizen. If he who pays a tax equivalent to three days' work has less right than he who pays a tax equal to ten days' work, it follows that he who has an income of one hundred thousand livres has one hundred-fold more right than he with only one thousand livres. It follows from your earlier decrees that each citizen has a right to contribute to the making of the law, and thus to be eligible for election, irrespective of distinction of fortune.'

Other Left Wing deputies succeeded Robespierre. Dupont de Nemours insisted that a capacity to conduct affairs, a matter upon which the people could be relied to judge for itself, should be sufficient qualification for election. Later, he pointed out that Rousseau himself would not have been eligible. Grégoire voiced his fear of the establishment of an aristocracy of the rich. All that should be necessary was the possession of a French heart. Thibault pointed out forcibly that the plan would exclude the majority of educated and enlightened men from election. He instanced particularly the humbler members of the Church. Barère extended Thibault's remarks to cover intelligent artisans and workmen. Target demonstrated that as nineteen-twentieths of the nation had no property, the great majority of workmen would be excluded. He also feared the establishment of a new aristocracy.

Prieur de la Marne continued the attack. He re-emphasised Robespierre's insistence that the whole plan was a flagrant violation of the Rights of Man. Defermont vehemently protested against society's being subjected to landowners, an aristocracy of the wealthy. 'How can it be expected that the poor will conform to laws to whose enactment they have not subscribed?' he asked. Legrand asserted that poverty itself was a title. Duport claimed that it was unjust to rate so highly a title which did not exist in the natural state.

But the Left Wing remained in the minority. The majority of the

Assembly were in favour of the property qualification, and an election in two stages, as providing a guarantee that the political control of the nation would remain in responsible hands. Their arguments were somewhat specious. Desmeuniers feared that were no contribution to be exacted, vagrants would be admitted to the primary Assemblies, for they paid no tribute to the State. 'The exclusion of the poor', he claimed, 'is no more than accidental. It will prove an object of emulation for the artisan (to secure electoral power) and that is the least advantage the administration will derive from it.' Populus favoured the clause requiring twelve months' residence, as he believed an intimate knowledge of local conditions to be essential for the exercise of electoral rights within a canton. A nameless deputy considered that the property qualification would debar the unworthy, such as courtesans, gamblers and financiers. Cazalès, it is true, expressed, not unexpectedly, his suspicion of the business man, the capitalist, and the banker. They were too cosmopolitan. They were liable to transfer their fortunes too easily. 'The landowner alone', he said, 'is a true citizen; he is chained to the land and interested in its fertility. It is for him to deliberate on the question of taxation.'

But even so prominent a member of the Left as Pétion de Villeneuve, whilst admitting that for long he had been in doubt as to whether the payment of a tax should be a necessary qualification for active citizenship, and that he had held the view that every citizen should partake of the *droits de la cité*, yet concluded that 'where the people is an ancient one and corrupt, I have noted the necessity of the qualifications proposed by your committee'. He did, however, draw a distinction between the electors and citizens eligible for election, and favoured capacity, as distinct from property, as the only necessary qualification for election.

Although on October 29th, the suggestions of the Committee were substantially adopted,[1] the Left Wing never ceased to advocate modifications of the electoral system right up to the end of 1791. Thus Robespierre, in January, 1790, was successful in showing that the whole province of Artois would be disenfranchised under the new electoral system, as direct taxation was there unknown. The Assembly, in this case, suspended the qualification of the *marc d'argent*, as in other places where direct taxes were not paid, until the position

---

[1] During the first revision of the Constitution the number of deputies was changed to seven hundred and forty-five, elected by eight-three departments, together with an unspecified number elected in the colonies.

had been regularised.[1] Under pressure, several other minor points were ceded. But, in general, the plan retained its original form.

A fundamental change, it is true, occurred in the qualification deemed necessary for an 'active' citizen to become eligible for election to the Assembly, as a result of the swing to the Left which followed upon the King's flight to Varennes. As a sop to the increasingly violent democratic outlook of many of the deputies, and to the scarcely veiled republicanism of Paris, the tax qualification for election to the Assembly was entirely removed, any 'active' citizen thereby becoming eligible. So much the Constitutionalists were, under stress, prepared to grant. But to preserve the supremacy of the Third Estate, they later proceeded to negative this concession almost completely by raising the tax qualification for election as an 'elector' by the primary assemblies to from twice to eight times the value of the *marc d'argent*. So great an uproar did this measure create,[2] however, that of necessity they were compelled to postpone its operation for two years.

It is noteworthy that the principle of capacity, as ensuring the true interpretation of the common interest, had led the Assembly to limit the vote not only to those adults who had reached the age of twenty-five years and were otherwise eligible, but also to men alone. The exclusion of women, indeed, was not a controversial matter within the Assembly.[3] Condorcet had advocated the grant of electoral rights to women as early as 1788, and again in 1790, when he published his article, *Sur l'admission de la femme au droit de cité*.[4] In the days of *l'ancien régime*, women who were proprietors of fiefs in their own right had been represented by proxy in the Estates General, but the Assembly was not influenced by this precedent, nor yet by the *Sociétés Patriotiques de Citoyennes* which had been established after the Revolution had begun. They were equally unmoved by the spate of petitions

[1] Dr. Renier points out (*Robespierre*, p. 59) that his enemies used this as a lever to convince the 'worthy citizens of Artois' that Robespierre was out to raise their taxes.

[2] As J. M. Thompson has pointed out (*The French Revolution*, p. 222), this piece of legislation meant that whilst an 'active' citizen could vote in the election of a mayor, a parson or a justice of the peace, the election of deputies, bishops, judges and departmental and district directors remained in the hands of a small propertied class. Thus, in the department of Loire-et-Cher, there were 200 electors only in a population of 275,000, and in that of Aveyron, 210 electors, although the population numbered 400,000.

[3] Cf. Gautherot, op. cit., p. 419.—'L'Assemblée Constituante ne songea guère à doter la femme des droits politiques.'

[4] The full text is quoted in Buchez et Roux, op. cit., Vol. IX, pp. 98 f.

and brochures on the question which circulated from 1789 onwards. Certainly, no debate appears to have taken place upon the matter.

The Assembly had thus succeeded in largely removing the legislative power in the nation from the control of all but a minority of wealthier citizens. By developing a 'representative general will' which reflected in theory the 'general will' of the nation, and thus paying lip service to the principles of the Declaration of Rights, and by refusing to admit that they were *mandataires*, the deputies had succeeded in liberating future Assemblies from any real dependence upon the will of the electors. In the suspensive veto, a means had been found by which, again theoretically, the 'representative general will' could at all times be brought into line with the 'general will'. Hence the Assembly believed that it had theoretically preserved the letter of the Declaration.

But by further justifying the creation of a body of active citizens, alone entitled to vote, on the ground that the true 'general will' could be ascertained only by excluding the unreasoned judgment of the illiterate masses, and by making the property qualification for eligibility for election so high that barely one twentieth of the nation could qualify, the Assembly had virtually placed all power in the State in the hands of a plutocracy of wealthier citizens. The Third Estate was thus protected from the growing radicalism of Paris and of its own Left Wing. In comparing the outlook of the Assembly in the July days with its outlook in the last days of October, there can be little doubt that the establishment of a narrow electoral framework was at least partly the result of mob violence, of the increasingly democratic outlook of the Paris Commune, and of the revolutionary ardour of the Palais Royal.

Compared with the extent of the suffrage at the time of the elections to the Estates General, the narrow franchise proposed by the Assembly was markedly illiberal, although not perhaps more so than that in England at the time. A measure of the general disapproval with which the plan was met in the country generally, however, was the decision of the Legislative Assembly, no more than eleven months after the Constitution of 1791 had been decreed, to establish what virtually amounted to universal suffrage, whilst the projected Constitution of 1793, although this never came into effect, was to go even further in proposing to eliminate altogether the system of indirect election to the Assembly.

CHAPTER IV

THE STRUCTURE OF THE LEGISLATURE

THE adoption by the National Assembly of the representative principle of government had justified the establishment of a legislative assembly, possessed of a 'representative general will' which theoretically reflected the 'general will' of the nation, and so preserved, equally theoretically, the principle of the sovereignty of the people. But the difficulty remained of formulating the structure of such a legislative corporation which fitted into this framework in a class-ridden country governed by an hereditary monarch.

By 1789, the necessity for the separation of the powers of government as a bulwark of freedom was widely accepted in France. Indeed, it had virtually become a dogma. General recognition of the fact that the sovereign power of the nation could be exercised only by delegation was accompanied by an equal recognition of the desirability of instituting such safeguards that the wielders of this power could never become tyrannical. The method of avoiding this danger had been clearly demonstrated by Montesquieu. *Pour qu'on ne puisse abuser du pouvoir*, ran the famous lines, *il faut que par la disposition des choses, le pouvoir arrête le pouvoir*. Arising out of a classic misinterpretation of the nature of the English parliamentary system, there can be little doubt that Montesquieu's description of the separation of powers was widely known in France,[1] and with the practical application of the principle in America before its eyes, the nation had clamoured for its institution in the years which immediately preceded the summoning of the Estates General in 1789. Not only was such separation widely demanded in pamphlet and *cahier*; it was a cardinal principle which the newly constituted National Assembly, as we have seen, hastened to embody in the Declaration of the Rights of Man itself.

On July 9th, 1789, Mounier had described the separation of the powers of government as essential. 'Particularly', he claimed, 'is this important between the judicial and legislative powers, for authority is dispersed, its various powers are invariably contradictory, and in their

---

[1] For a detailed examination of the influence of the *Esprit des Lois* on the National Assembly, cf. Saint-Giron's *Essai sur la séparation des pouvoirs*, pp. 101 f.

perpetual collision, the rights of obscure citizens are betrayed. The laws are openly despised, or rather, no two persons are agreed on what should be called the law.'

Mounier, and those other deputies who formed the Right Wing or Monarchist Group in the Assembly, advocated the separation of the powers of government mainly to restore equilibrium to the traditional government of France. As Champion de Cicé insisted, 'Up to now this vast and superb empire has never ceased to be the victim of the confusion and indetermination of powers'. But their outlook made of such separation a tentative and somewhat half-hearted reform, a mere patching-up of the historic monarchy. Whilst they were anxious to guard against any return of royal despotism, they were equally anxious to advocate no reform which would injure royalty itself.

The Constitutionalists were also convinced that the separation of powers was a necessary attribute of freedom. On July 11th Lafayette claimed that every government having as its sole aim the public well-being, this interest demanded that the legislature, the executive and the judiciary should be clearly defined, and that their organisation should assure the free representation of the body of citizens, the responsibility of its agents and the impartiality of its judges. The Comte de Virieu, speaking on the 28th, also showed that 'three powers exist which co-operate in the maintenance of society, the legislative power, the executive power and the judicial power. As soon as these three powers are united in the hands of a single individual or body, despotism reigns. If they are united in the hands of a tyrant, the nation can combat it, but where they become united within the hands of the nation itself, then the State will be torn apart, and no force will suffice to call it to order.'

Target, another prominent Constitutionalist, argued that 'the rights of man are assured only to the extent that the powers of government are distinct and wisely distributed'. Rhédon also thought that it was 'the wisely combined distribution of powers' which was the principal object of the Constitution. A nameless deputy gave it as his opinion that every citizen had the right to demand of society a guarantee of his rights, and this was impossible where the division of powers and of responsibilities was not assured. Le Chapelier in turn emphasised that the liberty of the citizens required that the different powers of government should be determined. Many other speakers of the Left Centre reiterated similar views.

Mirabeau also looked upon such a separation of powers as essential to liberty. But, as powers of government, they necessarily had their source in the sovereignty of the people, and he declared that, 'All power emanating from the people, all the different magistrates or governmental officials, in whom is vested any authority whatsoever, legislative, executive or judicial, must at all times render account to them.' To Mirabeau, indeed, the work of drawing up the Constitution meant little more than determining and classifying the powers of government in such a way that no one of them could ever become arbitrary or despotic. Thus all powers of government were necessarily to be subjected to the sovereignty of the 'general will' of the nation.

There is some evidence, however, that the phrase 'separation of the powers of government' had tended to become as much a *cliché* as had the terms 'the general will' and 'the sovereignty of the people'—an imperfectly understood phrase which had become a tenet of the current *mystique*. Many deputies seemed doubtful about its precise implications. Thus whilst Lally-Tollendal could assert that the Americans, by instituting a Senate, had created four powers of government, Mounier could describe the three powers of government as the King and the two chambers of the legislature. So vague were many of the deputies about the matter, that Rabaut de St. Etienne was led to complain of the lack of precision in terminology and to demand clarification before further discussion took place.

Primarily, in this chapter, we shall discuss the development of the principle of the separation of powers in relation to the structure of the legislative body itself. Later, in two subsequent chapters, we shall examine the application of the principle to the relationship established between the legislature and the executive and judicial powers respectively. Initially, in view of the increasing restiveness of the Paris mob, particularly after the removal of the Assembly from Versailles to Paris, it appeared very necessary to the deputies that a strong legislature should be established without further delay.

The problem of the structure of the legislative body had come to the fore during the debates on the establishment of the electoral system. Was the legislature to be a unicameral body, or was it desirable to secure check and countercheck of one body by another by establishing a Second Chamber which would fulfil the functions of a Senate?

To the Right Centre, as also to the more extreme Right Wing, the establishment of such an Upper Chamber appeared a *sine qua non*. The stability of the State necessitated, in their view, an instrument for tempering the opinions of an elected Lower House; such an instrument lay to hand in the formation of an aristocratic Upper Chamber constituted on an hereditary basis. Only in this way, they insisted, could hasty or ill-advised legislation be checked, and the King guided in his use of the suspensive veto. The case was put more clearly by Mounier. 'It must be asked', he said, 'if the King, inasmuch as he is a part of the legislative body, will not find himself ceaselessly exposed to a continuous restriction of his legitimate power by the union of all wills in a single Chamber. Suppose he gives way. Then, what will limit the powers of the Chamber? The people would be placed at the mercy of a tyranny. What if he resists? This would lead to intolerable interference by the executive power. What an alarming source of trouble this would be. The representatives of the people should regard the King as a bulwark against the Senate, and the Senate as a bulwark against the King. The Senate will at the same time safeguard the rights of the Chamber and those of the throne. The King will keep in check the two Chambers, the one by means of the other.'

Without such an hereditary Second Chamber, argued Lally-Tollendal, no fewer than three real dangers would emerge. Primarily, without a Senate, the Assembly and the executive power would crush each other. Three powers were necessary to maintain equilibrium in the State. Otherwise, a battle would rage in which one power would ultimately absorb the others. Secondly, a unicameral legislature would often be 'misled by eloquence, seduced by sophistries, and inflamed by passion'. And finally, not only would the Constitution itself be endangered by an Assembly which could vary it overnight, but any influence which the King might retain would be shattered by the uniting of all individual wills in a single National Chamber.

These, and similar arguments, were reiterated by other deputies of the Right. Precedent favoured a bicameral legislature. Had not the Estates General itself been summoned as three Chambers? Had not the Americans established two Chambers in Congress? Had not Montesquieu praised the English House of Lords ?

The Left Centre, as also the more extreme Left Wing, however, opposed any suggestion of the establishment of an hereditary Second Chamber, and in this they had the support of those members of the Noble Order who would not be eligible for membership of such a Chamber. How could an aristocratic Senate be established in view of the proclamation by the Assembly of the sovereignty of the people? Such a Chamber would, of necessity, be a creation not of the people, but of the King.   Many speakers referred to the period of the 'dead-lock', to the fight for the *vote par tête*, to their conviction that an aristocratic Chamber, apart from hindering and interfering with the work of the Lower House, would provide a suitable channel by which the King and his Ministers, denied the absolute veto, could bring pressure to bear on the representatives of the sovereign people.   In particular, Rabaut de St. Etienne poured scorn on any suggestion that the English system should be regarded as a precedent, or that it had relevance to the problem facing the Assembly.   'The idea of two Chambers (in England) did not originate in any attempt to balance political power', he asserted: 'it did not evolve as a means of retarding the onward march of the representatives of the people'.

The opponents of an hereditary Second Chamber were less con-cerned with theoretical arguments than with the danger of reconstitut-ing a reactionary element in the Government.   Here again, suspicion of the King was clearly in evidence.   As Lanjuinais remarked, 'On the ruins of that Nobility which has now been reduced to its rightful place in the scheme of things, there would be erected a more monstrous monument of aristocracy than that which previously existed.'   And Le Sillery was equally emphatic that 'Scarcely have we escaped from the cruel claws of one aristocracy, when we are in danger of falling, by our own errors, into the claws of another'.   Any idea of establishing a Second Chamber in which the King nominated the members would be 'one of those frightening ideas which it should no longer be possible to voice in the National Assembly'.

But purely as a means of checking unwise legislation, the idea of an elected Second Chamber had some influence in the ranks of the Left Centre Party.   The difficulty of its incompatibility with the principle of the sovereignty of the people could be overcome by ensur-ing that the Chamber was also representative of the nation.   The dispute which arose over this question had both a philosophical and a political character.   Some deputies were mainly concerned to secure an appropriate balance of power.   They feared the despotism of a unicameral legislature.   Other deputies were anxious to hedge against what they regarded as an increasing radicalism in the outlook of the Assembly, and particularly in the Jacobin Club.[1]   Finally, other deputies, with the support of the Left Wing, insisted upon a single Chamber as the only body in which the 'general will' of the sovereign nation could be ascertained.   Only in this way, they claimed, could

[1] Cf. Brinton, op. cit., pp. 144 f.

the original meeting of all the citizens in the State be reflected in the meeting of representative citizens in the Nation State.

Thus, within the Constitutional Group, Dupont de Nemours was a leading advocate of two popularly elected Chambers, to be elected at the same time by the same electorate. He suggested that three candidates should be elected in each primary assembly, the eldest of whom would enter the Senate, and the remaining two the Lower House. Then the Senate, 'composed of our equals', would review the legislation of the Chamber of Representatives, and either reject it or adopt it. In the event of differences between the two Chambers, the plans of the Lower House would prevail after three consecutive readings in the Senate had failed to provide a basis for agreement. Dupont was strongly supported by De Castellane. Other deputies advanced similar projects.

The strongest counter-argument to these suggestions was supplied by Montmorency, also a member of the Left Centre, who showed that if both Chambers were elected and composed on the same principle, they would not provide the necessary check upon each other. On the other hand, were they to be composed on different principles, a new aristocracy would be established. 'If the two Chambers are formed in the same way', he asserted, 'one of them will become useless. . . . If, on the other hand, their formation is not the same and the project of the Senate is adopted, it will re-create an aristocracy and lead to the enslavement of the people, above all where the Senators are immovable, or where they are chosen by the King.' Hence he concluded, 'Two Chambers are inadmissible, because of the barriers they will ceaselessly erect against the reform of abuses.'

The main argument for a single Chamber, however, was based on the teachings of the current *mystique* rather than on political grounds. Despite earlier recognition by the Assembly of the representative principle, the desirability of preserving the support of the masses appeared to necessitate reinforcement of the principle that all resolutions of the legislative body should be a true copy of the 'general will'. It was argued that any division of the legislature would destroy the unity of the 'representative general will'.

Several attempts were made to avoid this difficulty. In one sense the scheme of Dupont de Nemours had done so. Clermont-Tonnerre, Malouet and other deputies outlined similar ways of avoiding infringement of the common will. The most elaborate scheme was that of Sieyès, who attempted to show that the unity of the common will required only unity of decision, and not necessarily unity of discussion. All the advantages of a dual system would be preserved if the law were to proceed from a decision of the united Chambers. He visualised three such Chambers. 'It is evident', he claimed, 'that it is often wise to discuss the same question two or three times. There is nothing to prevent such a discussion taking place in three separate rooms, and before three sections of the Assembly. There would then be no danger of undue haste of decision, no repetition of actions based on errors of judgment or arising from seductive eloquence. It would suffice that a decision would be based on the total numbers of votes cast in the three sections, exactly as though the vote had been taken in a single Chamber. It would be necessary, of course, to count the votes *par tête* and not *par chambre*. There would then be no need to give the power of veto to anyone, for such a power would arise naturally where one section of the Assembly might judge it wise to delay reaching a decision. This would, in effect, have the same result as a suspensive veto.'

Nevertheless, despite such suggestions, the desire to act as closely as possible within the framework of popular thought, coupled with a healthy fear of the aristocracy which might yet succeed in sabotaging the Revolution, prevailed, and the Assembly, after further long discussion, ultimately decided in favour of a single Chamber. As Rabaut de St. Etienne insisted, in a final speech, 'The sovereign power is a single entity, as it is the general will of the nation. Hence the legislative power must be a single entity, for if the sovereign power cannot be divided, no more can the legislative power be divided. There cannot be two or three legislative powers without there being at the same time two or three sovereign powers.'

The Jacobin Club had favoured such a decision from the onset, and there can be little doubt that the leaders of the Left Centre were not unmindful of Club opinion. Jacobinism had become identified with the concept of the sovereignty of the people. 'There is only one legitimate authority, that of the people in its simplicity', maintained the Club in Neuilly-St-Front; 'it alone is good, because the people which exerts it is both active and passive.'[1] Hence many Jacobins continued to assert, despite the establishment of the representative principle of government by the Assembly, that the members of the legislature were never more than the *mandataires* of this sovereign people. 'The

---

[1] Dommanget, M: *La Révolution dans le Canton de Neuilly-St-Front*, p. 117, quoted Brinton, op. cit., p. 142.

Society', insisted another provincial club, 'penetrated with the natural and undeniable principle that all men are free and equal, maintains that political associations are the sole judges of the laws which should rule them, and that the rulers are but their *mandataires*, on such conditions and for such a period as pleases them.'[1]

Thus it was natural that Jacobinism should be associated everywhere with a single chamber. In yet another provincial club, for example, the members took an oath never to permit the establishment of a bicameral legislature.[2] At Melun, an explicit reason was given for a similar attitude. 'What really makes the sovereign is the union of all members of the State, acting and deliberating together. To divide this sovereignty is to destroy it. It can only produce a legal and legitimate opinion when it is formed into a single assembly. Diverse wills, manifested in partial assemblies, are often very different from what they would be in a general assembly.'[3]

The Constitutional Party and the Left Wing accepted this point of view. It still further removed the danger of royal interference in the affairs of the Assembly; at the same time it enabled them once again to identify their policy with the principles of the current *mystique*, and so increase their popularity with the masses.

The structure of the legislature being thus determined, the Assembly had next to turn its attention to the vexed question of the relationship which was to be established between the legislative power and the executive and judicial powers respectively. The position of the King having been settled as part of the legislative power, what was to be his relationship to the Assembly as head of the executive power, and as the royal fountain of justice? In the two following chapters we shall deal in turn with these twin problems, in each of which the doctrine of the separation of powers, demanded in so many *cahiers* and codified in the Declaration of Rights, was destined to receive a special interpretation.

---

[1] *Journal de Clubs*, No. 5.
[2] Libois, H: *Déliberations de la Société populaire de Lons-le-Saunier*, p. 46.
[3] Noviel, E.: La Société des Amis de la Constitution de Melun, in *La Révolution Française*, Vol. XLI, p. 335.

CHAPTER V

THE EXECUTIVE POWER

AS the body charged with the task of formulating a new Constitution the Assembly had, since the days of the deadlock, concerned itself with the task of shouldering the day-to-day legislative duties which had to be fulfilled during the constituent period. For although it had nowhere been clearly defined, the deputies had acted upon the assumption that during their period of office as a constituent assembly, all normal powers of government were concentrated in themselves. And in so far as the executive power was concerned, they had little choice in the matter. The country as a whole from 1789 onwards had little confidence in or respect for the *ci-devant* civil service or the King's ministers who controlled the chief offices of State. Equally the Assembly, suspicious of the Ministry as of Louis himself, were loath to place overmuch trust in conservative and often reactionary officials who could virtually sabotage its decrees. In order to safeguard the carrying-out of its measures, the Assembly had early been compelled to set up committees to supervise the administrative machine, as also to initiate the appropriate measures of reform.

Such committees included the *comité diplomatique* which dealt with foreign despatches and ambassadors' reports; the *comité des recherches* which issued warrants of arrest; the *comité d'aliénation* which dealt with land sales; the *comité des finances* which controlled the currency; and the *comité ecclésiastique* which administered Church affairs and later imposed the clerical oath. Such committees safeguarded the Assembly from possible sabotage of its decrees by incompetent or corrupt local administrators. By means of comprehensive *instructions*, the committees provided detailed guidance upon the interpretation and enforcement of such decrees.

It cannot, therefore, be a matter for surprise that in defining the constitutional limits of the executive power, the Assembly should have been influenced by its own experience, nor that it was loath to risk the placing of too much authority in the hands of men who could not forget *l'ancien régime*, nor that it should further insist upon retaining a supervisory rôle in its relationship with the executive. But at the same time it was necessary to have regard to the doctrine of the separation of powers, demanded in the *cahiers*, enshrined in the Declaration of Rights, and supported as an article of faith by the Jacobin Club.[1]

It was, indeed, with respect to the executive power that the question of the separation of powers became of the greatest moment in the Assembly. In defining and formulating the legislative corporation in terms of the 'general will' of the sovereign nation the Assembly had, in effect, marked out the ground for the conflict which was to arise over the position of the two remaining powers of government in relation to the representative body which had been established. Such a conflict was still further to widen the gulf between the three main parties in the Assembly.

Broadly speaking, the Right Wing and the Right Centre party were anxious to preserve to the King a very real power. Much influenced, as we have seen, by the teachings of Montesquieu, they were emphatic that the executive must be preserved from all undue influence on the part of the legislature. They were determined to secure the full implementation of Montesquieu's doctrine that 'All will be lost if the same man, or the same body of leaders or nobles or people exercise these three powers—that of making the laws, that of executing public resolutions and that of judging the crimes of, or differences between, individuals'.[2]

The extreme Left Wing was equally determined that all power in the State must ultimately rest with the Assembly, composed of the representatives of the sovereign people. All power was vested in the 'general will' of the nation. Hence the executive, as also the judiciary, must be subjected to this will. In a true democracy, all three powers met in the general assembly of all responsible citizens in the State. In the nation state, such a 'general will' could be ascertained only by a meeting together of the representatives of the people. It was therefore logical, in their view, to endow such a narrower assembly with similar powers.

Between the two extreme parties, the Constitutionalists were anxious to pursue a middle course. Afraid of the growing radicalism of the masses, and the increasing restiveness of the Paris mob, they were anxious to establish a strong executive, largely free from popular pressure. But the weakness and vacillation of the King, coupled with a constant suspicion as to his secret sympathies and reactionary

---

[1] Cf. Brinton, op. cit., pp. 142, 143.
[2] *L'Esprit des Lois*, Livre XI, Chap. VI.

tendencies, led them to avoid alienating too completely the executive power in the State. It was necessary for them to implement the doctrine of the separation of powers. But, equally, prudence compelled them to respect the principle of the sovereignty of the 'general will', a principle which had become the keystone of the retention of all real power by the Third Estate.

It was against this background, then, that the formulation of the executive power was to be worked out.

The *cahiers* had recognised that the King was the depositary of the executive power whilst at the same time declaring that the legislative power resided in the national legislative body. Again, the Assembly had already accepted the principle that the substance of power in the State could be divorced from its exercise in formulating the representative principle of government with its appanage 'the representative general will'. As the exercise of the legislative power could thus be vested in the Assembly, it appeared equally plain that the exercise of the executive power could be entrusted to the King. In either case the substance of power would remain with the people, and the sovereignty of the nation would remain unimpaired. This, however, would place the bearer of the executive power on equal grounds with the bearers of the legislative power, as both would owe their existence to the 'general will' of the people, and both were dependent upon it. Such a principle removed the King from his position as King in his own right. Were it to be implemented, the King would be head of the executive power by virtue of a right conferred upon him by the nation; he would become *un délégué obligatoire*.

With the exception of such die-hard extremists as remained in the Assembly by the end of 1789, such an interpretation of the position of the executive power appealed to the Right Wing. It preserved the King from interference by the legislature whilst at the same time avoiding any infringement of the ultimate sovereignty of the nation. But the Left Centre and Left Wing parties could not contemplate allowing the King such a free hand; it was necessary in the interests of the nation that the executive power must in some measure be subjected to the ultimate control of the Assembly.

How, in effect, would the King implement his power? By the issue of royal commands? By sending *instructions* to the administration? Would there not be real danger in permitting Louis to exercise too much power by virtue of his prerogative? Was the King to be permitted to initiate legislation? The Constitutional Party was determined that all royal authority must be curtailed and exercised only within predetermined limits.

Even the moderates in the Right Wing of the Assembly were afraid to go so far as to grant to the King the right of initiating legislation. Memories of the effects of absolute royal power were yet too fresh in their minds. As Mounier remarked, 'If the King were to send to the representatives of the nation edicts in which the various articles had been carefully prepared, the Crown would be able to circumvent our wishes, whenever it had previously been informed of them. It would lead to our losing the habit of making the laws ourselves, and resigning this function exclusively to the Crown. If the Government once gains the initiative, it will retain it always. More promptly aware than we are of what is happening in the Empire, it will always have prepared a suitable law; the people will become accustomed to receiving laws from this source, and they will thus be reduced to a state of subjection and dependence. A time will then come when the Ministry will introduce snares into its supposed benefits, and the nation will then deservedly lose its liberty as a consequence of abandoning its rights.'

Such arguments advanced by the Right Centre were strongly supported by the deputies of the Left. They were determined to ensure that no rival power to the Assembly could be established which might oppose the 'general will' of the nation as this was reflected in the legislative body.

The majority of these deputies were therefore anxious to utilise any measure by which the subordination of the executive to the legislative power could be achieved, and one loophole was ultimately perceived. The doctrine of the separation of powers implied the vesting of the legislative power in the Assembly and of the executive power in the King. But what exactly did the word 'law' imply? According to the Declaration of Rights, a law could be no more than a command of the 'general will' of the nation, which was binding upon all. From this it appeared that the King could publish no command which was of the nature of a law; he could not lay down any law by virtue of his prerogative. The implementation of such an idea would considerably limit his power of opposing his will to that of the legislature.

Mirabeau, and several members of the Royalist Group, opposed such a principle, which they believed would lead to the King's utilising underhand or illegal means to bring about legislation which he might consider at any time to be necessary for the benefit of the country.

They further argued that the King, as head of the executive power, was in a better position than anyone to discover loopholes in the laws, to discover the need for the introduction of new laws, the repeal of bad ones, or the amendment of defective ones.

But the majority of the Constitutionalists, fearful that their interests would be jeopardised by any such recognition of a royal prerogative, unanimously voted its suppression, and in this they had the support of many of the Left Wing deputies, including Pétion, who, it may be noted, argued that the royal prerogative would destroy the separation of powers in the Government. But it was in terms of the current *mystique* that the majority of deputies, including Lally-Tollendal, framed their opposition in claiming that as the laws were the expression of the 'general will', the King could not share in the initiative. It was thus decided that the King should be prevented from making any law, even of no more than a provisional character; he was permitted only to make proclamations in accordance with existing laws, which would ordain or further their execution. Further, he could send only *des ordres hiérarchiques* to the administration in pursuit of his task of executing such laws.

It was over the question of the King's ministers, however, that the greatest difficulties were to occur. For, on the one hand, the Assembly was compelled at least to pay lip-service to the doctrine of the separation of powers, whilst, on the other, the Constitutional Party and the Left Wing still relied on the fiction of the 'general will' to strengthen the power of the Third Estate.

The question of the Ministry was a complex one. It depended primarily upon who had the right to appoint or dismiss individual ministers. A strict interpretation of the doctrine of the separation of powers necessitated the placing of such authority in the hands of the King. But were this to be granted, it appeared that the legislature would lose all control over ministers of the Crown. Alternatively, to establish ministerial responsibility, it further appeared that the ministers must necessarily share in the legislative power. But this again might lead to corruption, especially where the King had appointed the ministers, and in any case would lead to the danger of the purity of the 'general will' being contaminated by the politics of the Court.

Thus the doctrine of the separation of powers and the theory of the 'general will' both seemed to imply the exclusion of ministers from the legislature. But the problem of subordinating the Ministry to the 'general will' of the people yet remained.

In excluding members of the legislature from participation in the executive, and vice versa, it is interesting to note that Montesquieu had gone further than Locke.[1] But although the influence of Montesquieu upon the Assembly in this matter was undoubtedly great, the deputies were more concerned to avoid the possibility of corruption rather than to interpret strictly the doctrine of the separation of powers. Their fear of ministers appointed by the King sharing in the work of legislation was not an unreasonable one. There were many deputies of the Right Wing who were watching the revolutionary tide with anxious eyes, whilst others were eager to curry royal favour. Again, experience of conditions under *l'ancien régime*, and of the King's vacillating behaviour during the early days at Versailles, had not tended to inspire confidence in the purity of the royal motive. Corruption of the legislature would be made easier were the King's ministers permitted to participate in its work and win over members to the royal point of view.

Again, American practice in this connection was not lost upon the Assembly, for in implementing a strict interpretation of the principle of separation in that country, the President of the United States was denied the right either to introduce legislation directly, or to do this through his ministers as intermediaries. His ministers had no seat in Congress.[2]

The question of deputies themselves being chosen as ministers by the King was first raised by Mirabeau on September 29th, when he asked the Assembly if ministers were to be excluded from the Assembly, if deputies were eligible for ministerial appointment, and if persons appointed as ministers from the ranks of the Assembly had to seek re-election when returning to that body. On November 6th he returned to the question, making an impassioned appeal that deputies should not be considered ineligible for ministerial appointment, stressing the advantages of the English system, and concluding by pointing out the dangers which could attend upon the machinations of a Ministry not subject to constant criticism by the Assembly. 'The influence of the ministers', he insisted, 'when this does not result from their ability and their virtue, may be due to secret manœuvres, to

[1] *L'Esprit des Lois*, Livre XI, Chap. VI. Cf. *Civil Government*, Book II, Chaps. XIII, XIV.

[2] Cf. Faÿ: op. cit., p. 264. Bergasse also bears striking witness to the influence of American precedent in this connection.—*Discours sur la manière dont il convient de limiter le Pouvoir Législatif et le Pouvoir Exécutif dans une Monarchie* (1789). This small pamphlet presents an admirable summary of the point of view of the Monarchists.

bribery, to hidden corruption, and the only deterrent which would affect their actions would be their liability to appear, as members of the Assembly, before an opposition which would have no necessary interest in supporting their views.'

As a secret counsellor of the King, as also one of the leaders in the Assembly, there can be little doubt that Mirabeau had ambitions of becoming head of a body of ministers similar to an English Cabinet. But other deputies were aware of these ambitions and were determined that at all costs they must be thwarted.

Mirabeau's chief opponents were Montlosier, Lanjuinais and Blin. It was the last-named deputy who made the fullest reply to his arguments. Could not the Assembly find talent outside the Assembly? It was the work of the deputies to act as intermediaries alone between the Assembly and the Ministry. The presence of ministers in the English Parliament was a main cause of the corruption found therein. 'There is', he said, 'in the English Parliament a corrupt majority which does not even trouble to hide its traffic in votes.' Hence, as the ministers in question had no true constituents, their so-called responsibility was a sham, for in reality they were responsible to no one. He concluded by asserting that 'If the ministers are present, one of two things must happen. Either they will defer to the wisdom of the Assembly, or they will succeed in influencing it. In the first case, they will needlessly abase themselves and so humiliate the executive power; in the second case, the Assembly will no longer be free and the nation will risk the loss of its liberty'. Finally, he demanded that were Mirabeau's point of view accepted in the Assembly, then members of the present legislature should be excepted from the rule.

Under no doubt that he was personally being attacked, Mirabeau sarcastically suggested that he alone should be prevented from becoming a minister. But Mirabeau was defeated. He shared in the suspicion with which the King was regarded. The debate had closely followed the military preparations of Louis, which had led directly to the events of the 5th and 6th October.

But granted that no member of the Assembly could at the same time become a minister, was it not yet desirable that the ministers should be admitted to the Assembly and share in the debates? Over this problem a further dispute raged. Mirabeau, supported by Le Chapelier, de Noailles and Clermont-Tonnerre, strongly supported the admission of ministers to the Assembly on the grounds that they might be readily consulted when need arose. This, they claimed, would lead to a fuller control of the executive power and would assist the Assembly in the difficult task of making the laws.

Strong opposition to the proposal came from the Left. D'André, Beaumetz, Blin, Roederer, Regnaud and Pétion de Villeneuve all spoke against it and expressed their fear of almost certain corruption. Robespierre made a particularly violent attack upon the proposal. 'Whilst ministers will be able to direct our deliberations', he exclaimed, 'it is to be feared that it is possible to visualise not only their ceaselessly affecting the purity of the legislature, but, moreover, their entry into the Assembly with a view to the consummation of the success of measures already taken outside it. It obviously tends to confound the executive with the legislative power, in that it confers on members who are clothed with this power the right to dispose of deliberation, and to exercise a direct influence on the making of the law.'

Bouche re-emphasised the doctrine of the separation of powers as a ground for the exclusion of ministers, although he, too, considered it important 'to provide against anything which may be attempted by the Court'. Other deputies supported him, but Thouret, Duport and Goupil de Préfeln argued that the Assembly was in danger of treating the King as a hostile power. This they believed to be wrong in principle. The executive had been created by the 'general will' of the people as had the legislature, and it was equally necessary for the preservation of freedom. Liberty was dependent upon the establishment of strong powers that would work together in harmony.

Tracy pointed out a further defect in the policy of excluding ministers from the legislature. 'The proposal', he claimed, 'is inconvenient. I do not speak on my own behalf, as I desire nothing and in any case am not likely to be sought for. But it will reduce the effectiveness of the executive power if it is compelled to choose its agents from amongst persons who are least familiar with affairs, whilst its principal functions necessitate the very best choice being made.'

After much further argument the Assembly ultimately decided that, in any case, ministers must be excluded from the legislature. The desire to ensure the supremacy of the representatives of the sovereign nation was the deciding factor. And the Assembly was supported in its decision by the fact that it fitted in with current *mystique*, in preserving ostentatiously the purity of the 'general will', whilst also being in accordance with a strict interpretation of the doctrine of the separation of the powers of government, demanded by the *cahiers* and reinforced by American precedent.

But having refused the Ministry a share in the legislative power, how was the Assembly to succeed in exercising control over the executive power? There was one possibility. Were a system of political ministerial responsibility to be set up by requiring the signature of a minister for all royal acts, such minister in turn to be made responsible for his acts to the Assembly, the executive power in this way might be harnessed to the will of the legislature.

It is interesting to note in passing that the doctrine of the political responsibility of ministers had not been recognised by Montesquieu, de Lolme or Blackstone. Neither had the doctrine been mentioned in the Declaration of Rights.

It further appeared clear that the Assembly could not itself retain the right of appointing and dismissing ministers, as this would have been too obvious a violation of the policy of separating the powers of government, which had been demanded by the 'general will' of the nation.

The question of the appointment and dismissal of ministers had arisen as early as July 13th, 1789, when the news of the dismissal of Necker reached the Assembly. Although a feeling of resentment was then aroused, the Assembly had no hesitation in asserting that the King had a perfect right to choose and dismiss his ministers. Target, Lally-Tollendal and Mounier were all emphatic about this right; Mounier, nevertheless, whilst admitting that, 'Certainly the King has the right to change his ministers', added that, 'At this moment of crisis, the representatives would betray their trust did they not warn the Monarch of the dangers to which imprudent counsellors had not hesitated to submit the whole of France'.

Two days later, however, a change of outlook occurred amongst the deputies of the Left Centre. This was reflected in Barnave's motion that the dismissal of ministers by the King did not 'merit the public support'. Mirabeau supported the view of the Left Centre in asserting that 'It is impossible to have confidence in the Ministry'. But Mounier and the Monarchists opposed the motion. Such interference with the rights of the King, they emphasised, was contrary to the doctrine of the separation of powers. It is possible that the matter would have been carried further had not the King, at this point, recalled Necker.[1]

Apart from some further discussion of the question on October

[1] Duclos (*La Notion de Constitution*, etc., p. 254.) considers that his recall was due to the hostile attitude of the Assembly.

20th, 1790, by Barnave, Cazalès, Beauharnais, Menou, Brevet and Clermont-Tonnere, in which the unpopularity of the King's right to dismiss his ministers was again opposed to an evident desire to maintain intact the doctrine of the separation of powers, and during which the Assembly seems to have moved some distance from its earlier declaration, the question did not rise again until 1791. On March 7th of that year, however, Desmeuniers, acting as spokesman of the Constitutional Committee, outlined a scheme whereby the Committee proposed to accord to the legislature the right of addressing petitions to the King, informing him that his ministers had lost the confidence of the nation. This, nevertheless, was not to interfere with the undoubted right of the King to retain them.

On April 6th, the Assembly adopted this proposal. But the Constituent Party was not yet sure of itself, and the Left Wing remained hostile to such a measure, in that they doubted its adequacy as a means of controlling the Ministry.

A further proposal of the Committee, however, carried the matter somewhat further. It was proposed that ministers should have the right of access to the legislature to defend themselves, and that they should be compelled to appear before it whenever that body should require their presence. In this way the ministers could be made responsible to the legislature, so it was believed, in that they would hesitate to embark upon a course of action which they would find difficulty in defending before the Assembly.

Such a proposal aroused opposition amongst those Left Wing deputies who most feared the reactionary tendencies of the Court. Barère particularly attacked that part of the proposal of the Committee which read, 'They shall be heard on all matters on which they may demand a hearing.' This, he believed, would give them a means of influencing legislation, which power could be directly conferred by the people alone. Citing Pitt's notorious influence in the English House of Commons, he asked, 'Gentlemen, do you not fear that in the National Assembly, a second Pitt may obtain a similar degree of influence, and lead the nation into similar dangers?' Would not the admission of ministers, he continued, enable the King to interfere directly with the legislative process? 'The King may demand that we meet a need of the country, he may ask for a law to be passed, he may demand that we decide matters on which we have inadequate information. But the ministers are present, with their supporters, to foster intrigues. Here they will argue and deliberate and secure votes with the ease of influential persons who hold the reins of power in their hands.'

Lanjuinais supported Barère's argument, but suggested that the difficulty could be overcome by a modification of the text of the proposal to read, 'The ministers shall not be heard, when they demand a hearing, except when the legislative body judges it desirable to permit them to speak.' Camus also spoke in favour of this amendment.

But Pétion believed that the security of the Assembly lay in the complete exclusion of the Ministry from the legislature. 'According to this article', he emphasised, 'the ministers may come to us and say that the execution of a law has created certain difficulties; in order to remove these difficulties, it is necessary to do such and such a thing . . . thus, not only do they have the powers of deputies, but they have privileges which no deputy can have.'

Robespierre also vigorously attacked any policy of admitting ministers to the legislature, and was so anxious to avoid any possibility of corruption that he further demanded that no member of the legislature should be permitted to become a minister of the Crown until at least four years had elapsed after his ceasing to be a member of that body. 'I have a simple proposition to make', he stated. 'A philosopher, whose principles you honour, said that in order to inspire more respect and confidence, a legislator should isolate himself from his work. It is the application of this maxim that I wish to propose to you.' Thence followed the above-mentioned demand. He again reiterated his earlier arguments that any such policy of admitting members to the Assembly was at once a breach with that concept of the sovereignty of the 'general will' that the deputies had accepted, and of the doctrine of the separation of powers itself.

Barnave, however, on behalf of the Constitutionalists, strongly supported the view of the Constitutional Committee. He pointed out that to limit the freedom of ministers to speak in the legislative assembly would considerably enhance the possibilities of corruption. Further, where the ministers were not consulted, the result would inevitably be the continued use by the King of his power of veto. 'In the government which you have established, you have instituted two powers', he declared, 'the legislature and the King. Now it is an established fact that if frequent use is made of the veto, these powers, invariably in opposition the one to the other, will finally destroy each other, and annihilate the Constitution. The veto is a necessity, but if it is invoked too frequently, it will be destructive.' An increasing number of deputies came over finally to this point of view.

Ultimately, the Assembly decided to admit ministers to the legislative body, and thus in effect it took a middle course. The King retained the right of nominating and dismissing the ministers of the Crown, and such ministers were to have a right of entry to the Assembly. But the King was not compelled to dismiss a minister on a vote of 'no confidence', although the Assembly had the right to address him on the subject. Thus the political responsibility of the ministry was not established. The concept of the purity of the 'general will' in terms of a representative legislature, the implications of the doctrine of the separation of the powers of government, both played a part in bringing about this decision. But the principal reason for the decision of the Assembly lay in the ever-present fear of corruption of the legislature by the reactionary elements of Court and aristocracy which provided a constant threat to the bourgeois citadel.

As a logical outcome of this decision the Assembly refused to grant to the King the power to dismiss the legislature which had been advocated by Montesquieu. This, in any case, would have still further threatened the supremacy of the legislative body. The Assembly, indeed, had recognised that a true separation of the powers of government necessitated a provision for the 'stoppage' of such powers in the interests of political freedom. For this reason it had granted the King a suspensive veto. But it was argued that such a power of dissolution was no more than a counterweight to parliamentary political responsibility. As this had not been set up, the right of dissolution was therefore unnecessary. But a speech of Le Chapelier revealed that once again the main reason for refusing this power to the King was suspicion of the royal motive.

On April 8th, 1791, the Assembly took a further step to establish the supremacy of the legislature, in reserving to itself the right to determine the functions to be performed by the executive. Desmeuniers, d'André, Barnave and other Left Centre deputies all spoke in favour of such a reservation, Barnave emphasising that, 'Whilst the Constitution has established the King as head of the executive power in the State, it has not given the executive the right to constitute itself. It is evident,' he continued, 'that upon the manner in which the Ministry is to be constituted depends its utility, that it may become absolute or nothing (*nul ou absolu*) and that it may be arranged in such a way as to elude any responsibility whatsoever.' Although the

motion reserving the right of the Assembly to determine such functions
was subsequently passed, it did not appear in the Constitution itself.

In pursuance of this resolution, however, the supremacy of the
Third Estate was still further reinforced by a series of limitations which
were imposed upon the powers of the ministers.   Thus it was decided
that, 'The ministers are required to present each year to the legislature,
at the opening of the session, an estimate of the expenses likely to arise
in their departments, to render account of the sums which have been
allocated to them, and to indicate any abuses which may have arisen in
the different parts of the governmental power.'

The very restricted powers which the Assembly was prepared to
grant to the King were manifest in many other directions.   The
agents of the administration were to be elected by the people.   The
King was limited as to the disciplinary powers which he could exercise
over his agents; in the case of their suspension, such action had to be
reported to the legislature, which could either confirm or reject such
suspension.

In vain the Right Wing deputies fought this subordination of the
executive power.   'Who is to be the judge', demanded Cazalès,
'between the National Assembly and the King?   Is the National
Assembly to judge?   In this case, the executive power will be judged
by the legislative power.   This is absolutely contrary to the Constitution, and completely opposed to the separation of powers.   Once the
executive power is made dependent, liberty vanishes.   The people,
unfortunately, cannot itself exert its powers; compelled to delegate
them it must balance the power which it confides.   In the centre of
them it reigns, it judges, it is sovereign.   But if one of these powers is
annihilated, the people is enslaved, it is no longer anything.   Thus,
every time that you place one of these powers in the ascendant, you are
traitors to that people of whom you speak so often, and whom you
serve.'

The Abbé Raynal himself was cited.   In a letter which reached the
Assembly on May 31st, and which was read by Ricard, he was quoted
as writing, 'You have kept the name of King, but in your Constitution
it is no longer of use and is even dangerous.   You have reduced his
influence to such a degree that corruption will usurp his authority; you
have invited him, so to speak, to fight a Constitution which constantly
shows him what he is not, but what he might become.   Here already
is an inherent vice in your Constitution, a vice which will destroy it if
you, or your successors, do not hasten to extirpate it.'

But such protests had little effect. The political security of the Third Estate necessitated the subordination of the royal power. The Constitutionalists refused to contemplate the establishment of strong powers outside the legislature, which might work to undermine the political framework which had been erected in the bourgeois interest.

In a large number of other cases, which have been admirably summarised by Duguit[1] and Duclos,[2] the legislature, by impinging on the territory of the executive power, in effect reduced it to no more than a function of the legislative power. As examples may be quoted the power of the legislature to order the alienation of the *domaines nationaux*, the regulation and policing of the Legislative Assembly and the Electoral Assemblies, the control of taxation, the making of orders relative to the responsibility of ministers and of decrees involving public prosecutions. And many of these strictly executive powers, thus vested in the legislature, were expressly excluded from requiring the sanction of the King.

So far as the power of declaring war was concerned, this also was reserved by the Assembly. On 'the formal and essential proposal of the King', a decree was to be drawn up and submitted for his sanction, where the legislature approved of the declaration of war. Where, because of the necessity for urgent action, the King had declared war, the legislature was to be immediately summoned to decide whether the war should be allowed to continue. In all cases, the legislature could require the King to negotiate a peace.

Hence the Assembly had decided that in order to justify the retention by the nation of the sovereign power, its chosen representatives must retain in their hands all ultimate authority in the State. And as provision had already been made for these representatives to be chosen from one particular class alone, this was tantamount to reserving to the Third Estate the means of controlling not only the masses, but also the King and the Ministry. The doctrine of the sovereignty of the 'general will' worked equally well in both directions. By the particular interpretation placed upon it by the Constitutionalists, not only were the people subjected to this will, but equally the King was powerless before it. It was in this way that the political supremacy of the Third Estate was assured.

[1] *La Séparation des Pouvoirs et l'Assemblée Nationale de 1789*, pp. 570 f.
[2] Op. cit., p. 272.

CHAPTER VI

THE JUDICIAL POWER

THE establishment of the judicial power was to prove a source of further difficulty to the National Assembly. On the one hand, its incorporation as a separate power of government seemed a necessary measure in the interests of the equality and personal freedom of the individual. For this reason, its separate identity had been demanded in the *cahiers*. Equally, the principle of popular sovereignty necessitated the delegation of power by the nation to a body of judges as it had necessitated such delegation respectively to the legislative body and to the King. But, on the other hand, it appeared clear to the deputies of the Left Centre and the Left Wing that there was a real danger to the political supremacy of the Third Estate in establishing a power which might impede the will of the Assembly, and partly through its power of interpreting the laws, and partly under the possible influence of subversive and reactionary elements in the State, might set up a will which could oppose the will of the legislative corporation. Constant suspicion of the King on the one hand, and fear of the ever-increasing radicalism of Paris on the other, made the Constitutionalists hesitate to embody a judiciary which would be completely independent of the legislature. Having taken steps to ensure that the 'representative general will', theoretically reflecting the 'general will' of the sovereign people, should always be in accord with the will of the Third Estate, and having, to all intents and purposes, harnessed the executive power to this will, it appeared madness not to take all necessary steps to subordinate the judiciary to the 'general will' of the sovereign people, as reflected in the will of the Assembly.

The Right Wing deputies, as also the moderates of the Right Centre Party, were not unprepared for such a manœuvre by the Left Wing deputies. Already they had seen on more than one occasion how the principle of the sovereignty of the 'general will', firmly embodied in the Declaration of Rights, could be twisted to ensure the supremacy of the Third Estate. Two lines of attack were open to them. One was to deny the necessity for such a third power, by arguing that the judiciary was in reality no more than part of the executive power. The other was to insist upon the complete independence of the judiciary, which would necessitate the King's nomination of the judges, who would subsequently hold office for life and be, in effect, irremovable.

Originally, indeed, so anxious was Cazalès to avoid any possibility of dependence of the judiciary that on March 29th, 1790, he went so far as to insist that it was quite unnecessary to reconstitute the judicial system at all, and he demanded a debate on this question. But the crushing condemnation of the pre-existing system in the revised report presented on behalf of the Constitutional Committee to the Assembly by Dellay d'Agier on March 27th was so devastating that Cazalès' outburst had little significance and his plea for a debate was overwhelmingly defeated.

The first attack of the Right Wing deputies opened on the following day. In an endeavour to secure the dependence of the judiciary upon the King as the fountain of all true justice, they asserted that Montesquieu himself had visualised no more than two powers of government, and had looked upon the judicial power as forming part of the executive power. In this way, by placing the judges directly under the King, they hoped to secure the judiciary from any undue influence of the legislature.

The remark of Montesquieu which reinforced this claim was his '*Des trois puissances dont nous avons parlé, celle de juger est en quelque façon nulle. Il n'en reste que deux.*' From this statement, these deputies succeeded in deducing that Montesquieu favoured the subordination of the judicial to the executive power.[1]

Nothing, of course, was further from the truth. The context of the remark shows that Montesquieu was arguing against giving the judicial power to a permanently sitting senate. '*La puissance de juger*', he wrote, '*ne doit pas être donnée à un Sénat permanent, mais exercée par des personnes tirées du corps du peuple, dans certain temps de l'année, de la manière prescrite par la loi, pour former un tribunal qui ne dure qu'autant que la nécessité le requiert. De cette façon, la puissance de juger, si terrible parmi les hommes, n'étant pas attaché ni à un certain état ni à une certaine profession, devient pour ainsi dire invisible et nulle, et l'on craint la magistrature et non point les magistrats.*'[2]

By entrusting the power to judge to assemblies of citizens sitting as courts at pre-determined times of the year, and separating when the

---

[1] Cf. Duguit: *La Séparation des Pouvoirs et l'Assemblée Nationale*, p. 14.
[2] *L'Esprit des Lois*, Livre XI, Chap. VI.

business was concluded, the judicial power could never usurp the functions of the two remaining powers. Montesquieu considered three independent powers to be necessary for the liberty of the subject, because that liberty was in danger only when all three powers were united against him—when one made the law against him, when another condemned him, and when a third executed judgment. But it was highly improbable that all three powers would thus conspire against the subject, as the interests of the three were not identical. Any two powers might do so, but not all three. As Montesquieu again wrote, '*Le chef d'œuvre de la législation est de savoir bien placer la puissance de juger, mais elle ne pouvait être plus mal que dans les mains de celui qui avait déjà la puissance exécutrice.*'[1]

Nevertheless, this classic misinterpretation of Montesquieu was pressed by those deputies in the Assembly who, in advocating two powers alone, clearly hoped to strengthen the royal authority. Cazalès alone correctly interpreted Montesquieu, but claimed that he was mistaken. 'I surrender only to truth and reason,' he exclaimed, 'and the one and the other tell me that there is not a single reasonable man, of good faith, who can recognise more than two powers. . . . When the sovereign has distributed all the powers, when it has determined the laws, and the means of executing them, what remains to be done? What could be the employment of a third power? Montesquieu for a long time exercised, with great success, the duties of a magistrate; he was greatly influenced by the outlook of his profession; he was misled in his opinions by the mixed state of the French Parlements, of which one may only conclude that they embodied a portion of both the legislative and executive powers, and not that they exercised a third power.'

Thus far, the arguments of the opposition had been based on Montesquieu's teaching. But other monarchist deputies had different reasons for supporting the fusion of the executive and judicial powers.

On May 7th, Clermont-Tonnerre had argued that in so far as civil and criminal jurisdiction was concerned, the judicial and executive powers formed a natural unity. His particular argument was based on the logical affinity between the two powers in this connection, but in supporting him, both Mirabeau and Mounier preferred rather to base their conclusions on the political ground that any division of the judiciary and the executive would result in each power being left too weak. In order that both powers should be strong, it was essential,

[1] *L'Esprit des Lois*, Livre XI, Chap. XI.

they claimed, that they should both be placed in the hands of the King. For this reason, it was asserted, France had always assigned the judicial power to the King. The Abbé Maury cited Rousseau on this point,[1] and then went further than Clermont-Tonnerre in arguing that any division of the executive power would turn France into a republic.

'What is the executive power?' he asked. 'Is it not the public force employed to execute the law? In republics this power may be divided. In monarchies it rests in the hands of the King. With regard to the judicial power, I claim that the influence of the monarch is not a usurpation; it is in the natural order of things, and secures the happiness of the people. . . . I conclude that the judicial power belongs to the executive.'

The Constitutional Party, however, with the support of the deputies of the Left Wing, retaliated in kind by correctly invoking Montesquieu's teaching in support of the establishment of the judiciary as a separate power of government; hence a unique situation arose in which both opposing parties made use of Montesquieu to justify their policies and he was quoted at length by many deputies during the course of the debates.

In point of fact, the original outline of the new judicial system had first been drafted by Bergasse, deputy for Lyons, who was a member of the Monarchist Group. In this report Bergasse had insisted, amongst other things, upon a complete separation of the judiciary from the legislature. He had, however, called into question the whole concept of the sovereignty of the so-called 'general will' of the nation.

'The law is the reverse of the simple will of the people. Wherever there exists only the will of the people, there is despotism. On the other hand, where there is harmony between this will and reason itself, there is law. Why, then,' he asked, 'do you claim that the law is the expression of the general will? Because a truly general will is always a will which conforms to the interest of humanity as a whole, and everything which so conforms to the interest of humanity can never be opposed to reason. . . . As the general will has always as its primary object the common interest, it is clear that you run the risk of being unable to discover the general will wherever men are liable to be deceived, for men who are deceived are invariably mistaken in their judgment.'

It was not possible, of course, for the Constitutionalists to accept

---

[1] Cf. *Considérations sur le Gouvernement de Pologne*, Chap. VIII.

such an interpretation, and Bergasse was replaced by Thouret on the Committee. Thouret's revised scheme was presented to the Assembly on December 24th, 1789, but the debate did not commence until March 24th, 1790. Thouret then opened his speech by listing comprehensively all the evils which were bound up with the administration of justice under *l'ancien régime*. He then went on to assert that, 'One of the abuses which perverted the judicial power in France was the confusion established in the minds of its depositaries between the functions which are proper to them, and the incompatible and incommunicable functions of the other public powers. As a rival of the legislative power the judiciary revised, modified or rejected the laws; as a rival of the executive power it interfered with its operations, held up its activities and disturbed its agents in the exercise of their duties.'

Hence, whilst the establishment of the judiciary as a separate power of government was essential, because of the dangers inherent in placing it under the executive, it was vital that its power should be controlled. 'A nation', he continued, 'which exercises the legislative power through a permanent body of representatives, can never leave to the executive tribunals of the law, nor submit to their authority, the faculty of revising the laws.' Finally, Thouret touched upon the vexed question of administrative jurisdiction. 'When the nation elects its administrators,' he concluded, 'the ministers engaged in the distribution of justice must in no wise concern themselves with administrative duties which have not been confided to them. The Committee . . . establishes the entire subordination of the judicial power to the legislative power, and separates very explicitly the administrative and judicial powers.'

In the debate which followed the presentation of this report, there was some confusion in the minds of many of the deputies about this question of administrative, as distinct from civil and criminal, jurisdiction. In a broad sense, it seemed to many of the deputies that the judiciary must fall within the scope of the executive power. The opponents of the institution of a third power of government insisted that there was a judicial aspect to every act of the executive power. But such a broad interpretation of the judicial power did not appeal to the Constitutionalists. They preferred to confine it within narrower limits, and thought of it only in terms of civil and criminal jurisdiction. To include administrative jurisdiction would be to open the door, so they believed, to interference with the judiciary by the executive power. It appeared safer to ensure a cleavage between these two powers by divorcing administrative from civil and criminal jurisdiction.[1] Once again, suspicion of the King and the Ministry was the deciding factor.

As Duport showed, on March 29th, 1790, a distinction was to be drawn between two kinds of laws—those which governed the relations between the citizen and society generally, and those which governed the relations between individual citizens. 'Judges should judge differences between citizens alone,' he declared.

But Duport, despite his allegiance to the Left Centre Group, was severely critical of Thouret's report. He, like the Right Wing, was opposed to the establishment of a judicial power, but for quite different reasons. He believed that a body of men—the judges—would be created who would not be sufficiently subservient to the 'general will' of the sovereign nation. The setting-up of such a power would be dangerous 'because it would give the judge an unnecessary authority by permitting him to judge disputes between citizens, an honourable and sacred function which would place those who exercised it above the rest of humanity. . . . All powers are established by the people for the people, and the people ought not to delegate its power where it can exercise it itself.' According to Duport, the people should undertake the judicial function of establishing the facts through a jury system. The judge then became no more than an official charged with the application of the law when the facts had been ascertained.

Chabroud and Durand de Maillane supported Duport. After further considerable discussion, however, the views of the Constitutionalists, as reflected in Thouret's report, prevailed, and the Assembly not only explicitly confined the judicial power to the field of civil and criminal jurisdiction, but established it finally as a separate power of government.

The next task which confronted the Constitutionalists, however, was how to organise the judiciary in such a way that its power was always subordinate to that of the legislative body, which alone reflected the 'general will' of the sovereign nation.

Primarily, it appeared that any subordination of the judiciary to the legislature would necessitate some control by the Assembly over the selection and appointment of the judges. And whilst it was

[1] For this they were severely criticised by Burke: *Reflections on the French Revolution* (Everyman ed.), pp. 205 f.

generally recognised that in a monarchical State the appointment of the judges was a prerogative of the King, yet it also seemed inevitable that where the sovereign power in the State was vested in the nation, the nation alone should have the right to elect the judges. Long and bitter discussion took place on this matter.

Duguit, it may be noted, considers that each separate power of government, being no more than a manifestation of sovereignty, must necessarily be conferred by the nation which is the sovereign power. The nation had elected the legislature ; the King held his office as head of the executive power by virtue of the common will of the nation. It therefore follows logically, he argues, that the nation, having decided upon the isolation of a third power, should similarly elect the officers in whom this power was to be vested.[1] Esmein, on the other hand, argues that this is not a necessary sequel to the adoption of the three-power principle; the head of one power can elect the head of another, as long as the powers themselves remain distinct.[2]

The National Assembly, as may be expected, was divided on this issue, the strongest supporters of the King's right to appoint the judges being those deputies of the Right Wing who had demanded the amalgamation of the judiciary with the executive power. 'In every political society', Cazalès insisted, 'there are only two powers, that which makes the law and that which executes it. . . . The application of the law is a dependency of the executive power, and if the executive power belongs to the King, it is for the King to name the judges.' The Abbé Maury supported him. 'Justice should be rendered in the King's name', he claimed. 'The nation itself cannot exercise its powers, and thus it has delegated them. If the executive power is extraneous to the Constitution, it is extraneous to the kingdom. If the King is without influence, you have no monarch, but a pensioner. The judicial power belongs to the executive.' Maury, however, was willing to compromise. 'The King should choose one of three judges elected by the people', he declared. 'His choice becomes a means of preserving the people from their errors.'

But this suggestion was strongly opposed by Le Chapelier. 'You have accomplished nothing if you are obliged to present three candidates to him', he asserted. 'The conscience of everyone must tell him that the man who obtains the preference of the Ministry is already the creature of the Ministry. If the judicial power is placed

---

[1] *La Séparation des Pouvoirs*, p. 71.
[2] *Elements de Droit Constitutionnel*, Vol. I, p. 544.

entirely in the hands of the judges, it is dangerous to put the judges in the hands of the King.'

Duport was equally concerned that the judges should be elected by the people. Only in this way could the principle of the sovereignty of the people be preserved, he declared.

At this point, Cazalès invoked Rousseau. 'A philosopher who cannot be suspect, a native of Geneva,' he pointed out, 'has said that Kings are judges born of the people; when they are no longer desirous of exercising justice, they confide it to their nominees. . . . Thus the King alone can nominate his judges.'[1]

A compromise proposal was submitted by Clermont-Tonnerre, who pointed out that a judge not only in reality held his powers from the people, as the source of the legislative power, but from the King also as head of the executive power. He therefore suggested that whilst the judges should be elected by the people, they should be instituted by the King.

Chabroud opposed this proposal. He, in company with other deputies, feared it as the first step to the establishment of a confederacy between the executive and judicial powers. Barnave went further and stated bluntly that such a proposal, if effected, 'would make the King master of the whole judicial power of the kingdom'. Le Chapelier also thought it would lead to the rights of the people being placed in the hands of the King.

The majority of deputies of the Left, nevertheless, saw in Clermont-Tonnerre's compromise proposal the only way in which the maintenance of bourgeois influence could be reconciled with that separation of the judicial power which the nation had demanded. At least the election of judges was a matter for the people, and this in itself considerably reduced the royal influence. Mirabeau strongly supported the proposal, as did Irland de Bazoges and Goupil de Préfeln, and it was this view, that the judges should be elected by the people but instituted by the King, which was finally accepted by the Assembly.

But the Assembly did not grant the King the right to refuse to institute the selected candidate. Hence it is clear that, in effect, a titular separation of the judicial power was alone established as the sovereign people could largely control the selection and appointment of judges, and thus the formation of the judiciary. This becomes even clearer when the question of the tenure of office by the judges

[1] Cazalès' reference was to the 'Gouvernement de Pologne', Chap. VIII.

is considered. Had it been the desire of the Assembly to separate the judicial power in any real sense from popular control, the judges would have been given office for life with secure tenure of their posts. But this would have been to jeopardise the power of the Third Estate.

Duport emphasised this point. In order to preserve the sovereign power of the 'general will', it was necessary that the term of office of the judges should be limited. Otherwise they would become 'proprietors of justice' and 'barriers to liberty'. Where the judges were nominated by the King, life tenure of office was clearly necessary, in order to separate them from undue royal influence. But where they were elected by the people, life tenure of office would establish a new 'judicial will' in opposition to the 'general will' of the nation.

Brocheton, d'André, Buzot and Roederer expressed similar views, and on August 16th the Assembly decided to limit the term of office of the judges to six years, although it was agreed that they should then be eligible for re-election.

There was further dissension in the ranks of the Constitutionalists over the question of the jury system. The Group had identified itself in principle with the argument advanced by Duport that the principle of national sovereignty necessitated the active participation of the people in the judicial function. The people, empanelled in juries, would ascertain the facts. Then the judges, chosen by the people and placed in office for a limited period, would enunciate the law. Thus, declared Duport, juries should participate in both criminal and civil trials.

Not only was Duport's suggestion supported by such members of the Left Centre as Chabroud, Goupil and Desmeuniers, but it was hailed with enthusiasm by such ultra-democrats of the Left Wing as Robespierre, Buzot and Pétion de Villeneuve.

But the majority of the deputies of the Constitutional Group were doubtful of its practicability in view of the prevailing ignorance of the masses. They were willing to accept the jury system in criminal cases, but they considered that the complexities of civil cases would prove too much for a popularly elected jury. Hence they insisted upon its introduction only in the former case, and despite an ingenious argument by Sieyès, who thought the difficulty could be got over by empanelling lawyers, to be selected by popular vote, in all civil cases, it was finally decided that juries should be set up only in criminal cases. Once again we find a conflict between the necessity for maintaining a doctrine intact and a foreboding that in the interests of the business and professional classes, it would be undesirable to hand over too much power to the masses so far as civil jurisdiction was concerned.

The question of any real separation of the judicial power turned also upon the extent to which the judges were to be subjected to the over-riding authority of another power. As before, the Assembly had to preserve the appearance of separation, which had been demanded by the *cahiers*, whilst securing that, in effect, such separation should remain largely formal in character. The question turned upon the right of the legislature to quash judicial decisions which did not meet with its approval, without making the power of quashing such decisions too obvious an interference with the judicial power.

Merlin believed that English precedent was the surest guide. 'The English', he said, 'have set you the example. They have confided the power of quashing a judgment to a single High Court.' It is not clear to what Merlin was referring, but if he meant the House of Lords, here was support for legislative interference with the judicial power. Goupil de Préfeln also emphasised that the power of quashing judgments, which might lead to attacks on the law itself, should be embodied in the legislature. 'To quash a judgment', he pointed out, 'is not to judge. Thus the right to quash a judgment should not belong to the judicial power; it emanates essentially from the legislative power.'

But many deputies viewed the absorption of such a power by the legislature with grave misgivings. They believed that it imperilled the liberty of the individual. Were a Court of Appeal to be established, they regarded it as essential that it should be included within the scope of the judicial power alone. 'The Court', said Barère de Vieusac, 'should be to the ordinary tribunals what the National Assembly is to the other powers.'

Robespierre, and the Left Wing deputies generally, however, were concerned to secure the sovereignty of the 'general will'. This seemed to them to imply that any doubt about the interpretation of this will in the Courts could be settled only by the representatives trusted by the people with such interpretation. 'It is on the general interest, it is on the maintenance of the law and of the legislative assembly that the Court of Appeal must pronounce', he asserted. 'As the legislative assembly establishes only the general law, the strength of which depends on its exact observation, if the magistrates can substitute their own will they will be legislators. It will thus be necessary to have a power of supervision which will restore the Courts to the principles of legislation. This power can only belong to the legislator, following principles which have been authentically recognised. It is for the legislator to interpret the law which he has made. It is thus necessary that the Assembly declare that to it alone belongs the right of maintaining legislation, and thus its own authority, be it by the quashing of judgments, or be it otherwise.'

Later, he again insisted that to place the power of quashing judgments anywhere but 'in the bosom of the legislature' would be to permit of individuals increasing their own prerogatives. They would not only attack the legislative body, but even the Constitution itself.

Le Chapelier supported Robespierre's view. He claimed that, 'the quashing of judgments in contravention of the law cannot be a right of the executive power . . . but a right of supervision which must be exercised by the legislature, for after this power of making the law comes naturally that of surveying its observance in such a way that, if it is possible, it will be on true principles that judgments contrary to the law will be quashed by decrees.'

But on this question there was more than one opinion current in the Constitutional Group. To many deputies, including Duport and Chabroud, it appeared that an appeal from a decision of the 'people', empanelled as juries, could be made to no body having a higher authority, as the 'people' itself was sovereign. The juries were not 'a constituted power', but 'the people itself'. Duport was prepared to admit a right of appeal on a question of law, as the judges might make a mistake, but never on a question of fact, determined by the sovereign people.

There was much further argument, but ultimately the Assembly again chose a middle path. It was decided that a Court of Appeal should be established by the side of the legislative body. This did not mean that it would act as a branch of the legislature. Its rôle was merely to be that of deciding on the legality of judgments given in the ordinary Courts. 'It can never go deeply into a case,' ran the decree, 'but only quash a judgment which has been made by a procedure in which the forms of justice have been violated, or which contains an express contravention of the law.'

In case the Court of Appeal might need to criticise the interpretation of law implied in any particular judgment given by a lower tribunal, it was further decreed that 'the question cannot be discussed without having been submitted to the legislative corporation, which will make a decree declaratory of the law, to which the Court of Appeal shall be required to conform.'

A further provision enacted that the Appeal Court was to be required to send eight of its members once in each year to the bar of the legislature, there to present a summary of all judgments made by the Court, 'beside each of which shall be an abridged notice of the case, and the text of the law which has led to each decision being determined'.

The extent to which these several compromise decisions vitiated the principle of the separation of the powers of government has been the subject of much controversy.[1] But so far as the National Assembly was concerned, the principle itself was not the primary factor. The Assembly was chiefly influenced by the fear that a power might be established which would detract from the authority of the legislature. Its eyes were fixed rather on the preservation of bourgeois supremacy than on any strict interpretation of the doctrine of the separation of powers. This was again evidenced by the refusal of the Assembly to grant to the King a right of pardon.

Duguit claims that in reaching this decision the Assembly was, in fact, animated by a desire to interpret strictly the principle of separation,[2] although Esmein does not agree that this was necessarily implied by its decision.[3] It was, however, fear of establishing within the executive power a prerogative which was outside the control of the legislature that decided the issue.

Thus the demand of the *cahiers* for the establishment of a separate judicial power was met by the setting-up of a titular or subjectively separated judiciary. The Assembly avoided reaching a conclusion in accord with such a strict interpretation of the principle of separation as that, for example, advanced by Duguit. They did not completely carry out the system advocated by Montesquieu. Once again their decisions reflected their great anxiety to retain at all costs the supremacy of the will of the Third Estate.

The doctrine of the sovereignty of the 'general will' had once again served the Constitutionalists well. Having vested the interpretation of such a will in an assembly elected by the bourgeoisie—the 'active' citizens—they had successfully avoided the possibility of any undue

[1] Cf. Esmein, op. cit., Vol. I, pp. 575 f.
[2] Op. cit., p. 99.
[3] Op. cit., p. 548.

opposition or interference emerging from either the King and his ministers on the one hand or from suborned judges on the other. At the same time, popular revolt could at any time be interpreted as a refusal to accept the 'general will' of the nation as discovered by its elected representatives.

But in order that this very principle of the sovereignty of the people might be preserved, it was necessary to provide for revision of the Constitution, for the nation had the sovereign right to change the Constitution should it so desire. Indeed, as we have seen, it was upon this right that the assumption that it could delegate the exercise, as distinct from the substance, of its power had been based. In the following chapter, therefore, we shall turn to this question of revision.

CHAPTER VII

THE CONSTITUTION-MAKING POWER

THE Assembly had succeeded in justifying their adoption of the representative principle and of a limited franchise, in terms of the current *mystique*, only by invoking the share of each citizen in the constituent power. As sovereignty had been declared to reside in the 'general will' of the mass of the people, it was clear that they possessed this power, for it was a natural concomitant of sovereignty which even the bourgeoisie could not bring themselves to deny. The problem of the constituent power, therefore, so far as they were concerned, was how to guide this inalienable right of the people into channels which would be of least danger to their own particular interests.

By their adoption of the representative principle, the Assembly had succeeded in creating a 'legislative will' which in practice embodied the sovereign power. By their further success in limiting the franchise, they had turned this 'legislative will' into what virtually amounted to a 'bourgeois will'. But the validity of their action turned ultimately on two further assumptions, that they had the right to embody such a 'legislative will', and that they reserved to the people as a whole the constitution-making power.

About the first assumption, no argument could arise. The power of drawing up a constitution for their country had been granted to the Assembly by the great majority of the *cahiers*; indeed, in many cases the vote of the taxes had been made to hinge upon their successfully completing this very task. Reubell, in particular, was emphatic about their possessing this power. 'We are the constituent body,' he declared, 'and consequently a national convention.'

But given the power of the Assembly to formulate a constitution, it was clear that the second assumption, that the people retained the constitution-making power, could be interpreted only as a right on their part to modify or extend from time to time the constitution which the Assembly had itself completed. Thus it could be argued that the possession of this power by the people implied no more than a right to initiate changes in an existing charter. Hence the funda-

99

mental task of the Assembly was to provide a means for the periodical revision of the Constitution, and thus to implement the Declaration of Rights, whilst ensuring that any machinery proposed for the carrying-out of such revision should not be capable of operating to the detriment of its own primary interests.

The Assembly had early drawn a distinction between 'fundamental' and 'ordinary' laws, and thus between the constituent and legislative powers. It had further, as has been noted, developed the view that whilst all power resided in the people, the people were active only in exercising the constituent power. The exercise of the legislative power was held to have been delegated to the representative corporation, but only on the specific assumption that the nation in fact retained this power of modifying the Constitution. As the Constitutional Committee, which reported on July 9th, 1789, declared, 'A Constitution is a precise and constant form of government . . . if this does not derive from the will of the people clearly expressed, it has no constitution. . . . We distinguish amongst the objectives which have been recommended to us, those which belong to the Constitution, and those which may properly form the basis of the laws. This distinction is easy, for it is impossible to confound the organisation of the powers of the State with rules emanating from the legislative body '

The reasons for the Assembly's insistence upon such a division between the legislative and constituent powers may be traced to varying sources.

Primarily, there was the purely political consideration that the legislative body could not possess the constituent power, because any such union of these two powers would destroy equilibrium within the state. Pétion de Villeneuve, in particular, emphasised this argument in basing his conclusions upon the necessity for a separation of powers. For where these two powers were not separated, he asserted that the legislature would become master of the executive and the judiciary.

The principle of the separation of the legislative and constituent powers had also been popularised by American practice, of which Lafayette, the de Lameths and de Noailles were enthusiastic interpreters. Lafayette particularly had emphasised that the American States had all established conventions to provide for changes in their Constitutions. Condorcet, Turgot and Mably had all commented upon and criticised American practice in this connection, and the many references to that country which occurred during the debates are an indication of the familiarity of most of the deputies with transatlantic procedure. The special contribution of America to French political thought lay partly in the determination of its people that a special organ must be responsible for constitutional matters. The electors of Massachusetts, for example, had rejected a draft constitution, which had been drawn up by the legislature, on the ground that such a work should have been carried out by a specially appointed body.

It may be noted that Duclos is opposed to too much emphasis being laid upon such American influence. 'It is difficult to believe', he declares, 'that the example of the American States could suddenly outweigh the mass of traditions which had accumulated over so many centuries in the minds of Frenchmen.'[1]

But as we have seen, such separation of the two powers was further an integral part of the Assembly's effort to interpret the current *mystique* in terms of the interests of the bourgeoisie. Their adoption of the representative system necessitated such a separation for its justification, as did their establishment of a limited electorate. And so successfully had they formulated this policy that so ardent a disciple of Rousseau as Salles could exclaim, 'The sovereign power is indivisible. Where it exists, it exists as a single entity. The power to act may be divided . . . but the power to will, never.'

The Assembly was thus compelled to face the question as to how a separate, constituent will could be embodied in such a way as to remain distinct from the legislative will of the representative corporation. For, in terms of the current political thought, as also having regard to the eighteenth-century idea of legislation as a fundamental act rather than a continuing process, it was identical with the 'general will', but this identity merely served to bring into prominence once again the very difficulties which had been so recently overcome in connection with the formulation of the legislative power.

Such a problem could not have arisen in a pure democracy, for the body of citizens there formed equally the constituent as also the legislative power. But in delegating the latter, the Assembly had been forced to justify its action by providing for popular control of the former, and such control was equally difficult to implement in practice.

There was one possibility. The adoption of the representative principle had freed the legislature from direct control by the people.

[1] *La Notion de Constitution dans l'Œuvre de l'Assemblée Constituante de 1789*, p. 27.

The legislative will did not, therefore, necessarily correspond with the 'general will'. This being so, could not the constituent will be made to reflect much more directly the 'general will' of the nation? Many deputies thought so. They visualised the creation of a constituent convention to initiate changes in the Constitution demanded by the people. But each deputy elected to such a convention was to be subjected to an imperative mandate on the ground that only thus could the 'general will' of the nation hope to find its true expression.

Such demands, however, opened up exactly the same dangers to bourgeois supremacy which had been visualised before. To place the Constitution at the mercy of the masses was a danger second only to that of their interfering with the legislative process itself. But any attempt to deal with the question on the lines upon which the legislative problem had been solved would not only have vitiated the spirit of the Declaration of Rights, but would have placed a weapon in the hands of the radicals, already restless because of the restriction of the electoral system, which would have enabled them to appeal to the people in terms of the popular philosophy of the day. At all costs, the bourgeoisie had to identify themselves with the current political propaganda.

Hence it appeared, allowance being made for the impossibility of collecting all the people together, that the constitution-making power must be vested in a popularly elected convention, and that any citizen or group of citizens should have the right to demand the summoning of such a convention. This much the Assembly was compelled to allow.

As it happened, the deputies had reached this point in their deliberations on the revision of the Constitution when the dramatic news was received of the escape of the King and the royal family from the Tuileries.

Louis XVI had never accepted the position which had been forced upon him by the events of 1789. Although the inherent weakness of his character and a possibly genuine desire to acquire the popular regard of his subjects had led him time and time again to pay lip service to the principles established by the new régime, and to represent himself as in complete accord with its doctrines of national sovereignty and a monarchy based on the 'general will' of the people, he had, as the months went by, sought for opportunities to place himself outside the authority of the National Assembly. He had accepted the *fait accompli* of the capture of the Bastille on July 14th, 1789, and had

removed his troops from Versailles. He had smiled upon and even
blessed the women who had dragged him from Versailles to the
Tuileries in October of that year. He had been present at the
Festival of the Federation held in the Champ de Mars on July 14th,
1790—a festival which had been a day of triumph for Lafayette but
a day of eclipse for the King. But the Court, as early as October 5th,
1789, had urged upon him the necessity of his removing himself to
the provinces, away from too close a proximity to Paris. Mirabeau
had been implicated in this design.[1]

But Louis had shrunk at the possibility of civil war. Another plot
for a royal flight had led to the trial of Augeard, the private secretary
of Marie-Antoinette, and of the Marquis de Favras. Throughout
1790 and 1791, Mirabeau, in secret correspondence with the Court,
had never ceased to emphasise the necessity for the King's escape from
the growing influence and power of Paris. In April, 1791, Mirabeau
died, discredited and disillusioned. And at long last, within little
more than two months of this event, the King yielded to his advisers,
and, accompanied by the royal family, made the attempt to escape to
the frontier, where forces had been gathered by the Emperor Leopold
of Austria to assist in the restoration of the Bourbon dynasty to its
pre-revolutionary position.

It is probable that the final straw which led to Louis' decision to
flee the country was his enforced acceptance of the Civil Constitution
of the Clergy, which had brought upon him the condemnation of
Rome and had led, within the country, to a schism and the beginnings
of a counter-revolutionary movement. This measure had caused
equally deep divergencies of opinion in the Assembly, already dis-
tracted by the intolerable difficulties of administering the programme
of land settlement, with its thorny questions of compensation, and by
the complex problems brought about by inflation, high prices and the
resultant speculation. The Groups within the Assembly were more
and more tending to become Parties in the sense in which it is justifiable to use that term of the Legislative Assembly of 1792. Already
the intolerance of 1793 and the disillusion of 1794 were becoming
apparent.

In Paris, the growing suspicion of the King had been closely paral-
leled by an increasing suspicion of the Assembly. It appeared to
the masses that the ideals of 1789 were being lost, that the alliance of

[1] He had sent a letter to the Comte de Provence urging him to advise Louis to
make his escape, preferably to Rouen—rich, royalist and ecclesiastical.

la haute bourgeoisie with the monarchy would mean no more than an exchange of masters—the creation of a plutocracy in place of an aristocracy. Such fears had been accentuated by the attitude of the Assembly to the royal 'veto', to the question of a Second Chamber, and to the implications of the *Loi Chapelier*.[1] The narrowness of the franchise had embittered public opinion, despite the care which the Assembly had taken to justify it in terms of the current *mystique*. Now, the flight of the King to Varennes brought to a head all this ill-concealed suspicion which had been growing for two years. There was general alarm as to the extent of the foreign intervention which was now hourly to be expected. In such an atmosphere, there can be little reason for surprise that Paris should have moved to the Left, and for the first time the word 'republic' should have been heard on the lips of the people.

The Press was virtually unanimous in demanding the establishment of a new form of executive power in place of the King. It is true that a minority of the newspapers alone used the word 'republic', but the writing on the wall was clear. Pamphlets advocating republicanism circulated widely. Paine nailed a summary of his 'Rights of Man' to the door of the *Manège*. The branches of the Cordeliers Club, acting chiefly at the instigation of Marat, openly spread republican propaganda. The crisis was at hand.

The Assembly acted with dignity. Its first action was to suspend the King from his royal functions. Indeed, the Assembly had so far assumed the responsibilities of the executive power, through the functioning of its various committees, that the change, in point of fact, was of little immediate significance. From June 26th until September 14th, when the restored King accepted the Constitution, the nation was virtually a republic.

Louis, having been intercepted at Varennes, within twenty miles of the frontier, was met on his return by Barnave and Pétion, who accompanied the royal family back to the Tuileries. A rapid decision as to his fate was necessary. The danger of a final breach between the Assembly and the capital was never closer.

But the reasons previously detailed for the Assembly's decision to safeguard the monarchy were now reinforced by two further dangers. The deputies realised that any attempt to dethrone the King would lead to an invasion of the country. And equally it was recognised

---

[1] Passed by the Assembly to safeguard the new régime from revolutionary factions and justified in terms of the 'general will' of the nation.

that any such attempt would lead to a crisis in which the labours of the Assembly for more than two years to formulate a Constitution designed to ensure bourgeois supremacy would be thrown into the melting-pot and possibly replaced by a more liberal and popular charter.

Hence the decision of the Constitutionalists, taken in the town house of La Rochefoucauld, to reinstate the King. The argument adopted to justify bourgeois policy in the light of popular opposition was that of the inviolability of the King. This argument was first introduced in the Assembly by Muguet de Nanthou on July 13th. The Left Wing was sceptical. Brissot scornfully asked how Louis could sin when the King could do no wrong. Robespierre branded such inviolability as a myth. Grégoire emphasised that any claim to inviolability on the part of the King was destroyed by Louis' denunciation of the Constitution.

The decision of the Constitutional Party to restore to the King his royal functions was reinforced, however, by a series of brilliant speeches from Barnave. He insisted that the Constitution must be completed if anarchy were to be avoided. He might have added, 'and the interests of *la haute bourgeoisie* maintained'. After a series of stormy sessions, it was decided to reinstate the King as soon as the Constitution had been completed, his acceptance thereof to be a condition of his reinstatement.

Thus it became immediately imperative not only to define the limits of that power of revising the Constitution which was itself the depositary of the constituent power, but to draw together and codify the scattered constitutional legislation which had been passed piecemeal during a period of more than two years. In order to expedite this task, a specially appointed Revisional Committee was attached to the Constitutional Committee which had hitherto been responsible for the formulation of the constitutional legislation of the Assembly.

The Joint Committees reported on August 29th, 1791, when Le Chapelier rose to place before the deputies what he described as 'the completion of our task—less the fruit of our reflections than the results of opinions assiduously collected'. He then proceeded to outline the joint views of the Constituent and Revisional Committees on the procedure to be adopted for the amendment of the Constitution. The Committees, he said, were anxious that two important principles should be admitted. These were that the nation had an imprescriptible right to revise and perfect its constitution, and that every constitution must contain within itself not only the desire but the means of

H

attaining the greatest degree of perfection; but this latter should, both in principle and in so far as its consequences were concerned, be employed with circumspection, for under the pretext of perfecting a constitution, its foundations might be so undermined that revolution would perpetually succeed revolution.

Le Chapelier then showed that four means of attaining these ends had been considered by the Joint Committees.

Primarily, they had examined the possible establishment of a general convention which would examine and revise the Constitution, which would be an all-powerful body, having the right to change it entirely, and which would thus be invested with all power which the Assembly itself had had, and which it had exercised. The objections to this scheme, however, were that the establishment of such a convention would 'cause credit to be annihilated, hold up commerce, interfere with the circulation of money, and whilst not perhaps causing a revolution, would create that fear which might result in one. It would put capitalists to flight, and cause red hatreds and divisions to be reborn within the country.' Apart from such obvious disadvantages, Le Chapelier went on to point out that there remained the basic difficulty of fixing a date for the convocation of such a national convention. Were it to be postponed to a relatively distant date, hope would be stifled, and factions, which ought to be crushed, perpetuated. As there would be little hope of more than distant reform, violent methods would be used. On the other hand, the fixing of an early date would result in the preservation of the various parties then in being; factions would be preserved intact, and disorders would continue.

The second proposal which had been examined by the Committees was that for the establishment of periodical conventions. This, Le Chapelier asserted, amounted in reality to the same thing. It was, in effect, the American system, which suited 'neither the form of our government nor the extent of our territory'. In America, the government was composed of a general association representative of small republics, between which there was a federal pact. There, a constituent convention, examining the Constitution of that country, would find a very extensive territory, few inhabitants and wise and peaceful customs. There, such an examination of the Constitution would not cause a revolution, but would prevent one. In France, on the contrary, where all men were, to some extent, crowded together; where the population was enormous; where change was desired for its own sake with a peculiar avidity; where passions were kept alive and characters were petulant; where the spirit of the nation was wont to overrun its own possibilities, periodical constituent assemblies would always be a time for revolution.

Having thus disposed of these two schemes, Le Chapelier turned to the third, that of prescribing formulae alone for the convocation of such a constituent assembly. Again he showed that the Committees were fearful of the perpetuation of existing parties, and of the political influence of the Clubs. 'In seeking to acquire the majority necessary for the summoning of a constituent convention', he said, 'there would be great upheavals, and public tranquillity would be disturbed; in the shortest possible time a factitious majority would call a revisional assembly to examine the Constitution, before experience has had time to enlighten them upon the advantages or faults of any one of the parties.'

The fourth alternative was the one to which the Committees were prepared to lend their support. This would involve the institution of an Assembly of Revision, which would have powers only to examine whether the Constitution had been strictly adhered to by the constituted powers, and to regulate any points on which reform may have been demanded. The plan proposed that such a revisional committee should meet at fixed times, or suggested conditions alone by which the establishment of such an assembly might be demanded. The right to so demand it was to be accorded to the citizens or to the constituted powers (that is to say, the legislative body and the King) only, thus enabling the petitions of the citizens and the requests of the constituted powers to be considered together.

In order to further this object, the Committees had produced the following scheme:—

Considering that the nation has the inalienable right of revising, reforming and changing both the system of its constitutional laws and the act of association itself, it is thus necessary, at the same time, for the general good of all, that the representatives of the nation require in its name obedience to the laws which they have decreed and approved, that they indicate a sure and prompt method of reforming them, and that they profit in this from the help which the nation may draw from the virtues, the genius and the experience of which these laws must become the source and object.

It is thus necessary only that the forms by which such opinions may be made known should be fixed in such a way as not to cause mistakes, to prevent tumultuous movements or irresponsible deliberations from taking upon themselves the imposing character of the 'general will', and to determine a period during which this will may be examined, a period which must not be so distant that the nation suffers from vicious parts of its social organisation, nor yet so soon that experience has not the time to provide its salutary lessons, or that the party spirit, the memory of ancient prejudice, would take the place of reason and justice, by which the citizens should henceforth be guided.

Finally, in the belief that the fixing of the period of delay and the determination of forms ensuring the reflection of the national will, in directing all ideas towards the common good and the perfection of the social organisation, have the happy effect of calming all agitations of the present time, and of insensibly leading all spirits to the peaceful pursuit of the public well-being, the following articles are decreed. . . .

The twenty-six articles which followed embraced both details of the formation of the Convention of Revision, and the duties which it was to be called upon to perform. The first such convention was to be summoned in 1800, and was to be made up of 249 deputies elected from each department, together with the legislative assembly itself. Its duties were to consist in ascertaining whether the constituted powers had kept within the limits laid down in the Constitution, and if not, in restoring the position, and in pronouncing upon the requests and petitions of citizens for constitutional reform, but only where these demands had been approved by the legislative body and sanctioned by the King. Where such approval had not been given, and either the King or the legislature had stated their motives for refusing such approval, after a lapse of eighteen months, and providing that at least three-quarters of the Departments put forward similar demands, the concurrence of the legislative body and the King was to be no longer necessary, and the reforms demanded could be submitted to the Committee of Revision as a matter of right.

By means of the popular election of a revisional convention, pledged to consider schemes which any citizen was entitled to put forward as of right for the amendment of the Constitution, the Joint Committees thus believed that they had succeeded in identifying, in principle, the constituent power with the 'general will' of the nation. But, clearly, safeguards had to be introduced by which the primary interests of the bourgeoisie would be protected. This could be done, it appeared, only by placing the exercise of the constituent power itself at the discretion of the constituted powers, themselves the stronghold of bourgeois supremacy.

The fiction of the 'general will' was to be preserved partly by granting to every citizen the right of petition, and partly by establishing a popularly elected convention, theoretically bound by the will of its electors; which, in co-operation with the bourgeois legislature, would proceed to isolate, or rather disentangle, the true 'general will' from a mass of conflicting suggestions.

But in order to circumvent the jealousies of the Clubs, and to avoid the ever-present danger of the subversive activities of enemies of the Revolution, misguided sectional interests and the like from subjecting the Constitution to continued attack, two particular safeguards were introduced. The first was the postponement of the summoning of the Convention of Revision until 1800. The second was the placing of the initiative in the hands of the legislature and the King.

The first safeguard had no philosophical justification; it was purely a political measure. But the second was to be justified, in terms of the current *mystique*, in that it provided the time necessary to ensure the complete generality of the national will, and to recall the representative will into harmony with it. In an ultimate sense, the sovereignty of the people was preserved.

Such was the plan submitted by the Joint Committees. Its virtue was that it did provide a means by which the hypothetical 'general will' of the nation could be ascertained. Its vice, in terms of the popular political thought of the times, was that it hedged round and hindered by every possible means, short of opposing the teaching of the current *mystique* itself, the methods by which this end was to be brought about.

As is to be expected, the plan was subjected to attack from both the Right and the extreme Left Wing Groups in the Assembly. Malouet led the opposition of the deputies of the Right. Primarily, he criticised the suggestion that no revisional convention should be summoned before 1800. This, he claimed, was tantamount to accepting the Constitution as incapable of improvement over a lengthy period of time, and took no account of any 'essential vices or inconveniences in the Constitution' which might from time to time become apparent. In any case, he believed that periodical conventions were admissible only in countries where the Constitution had stood the test of time, and truly reflected the 'customs, habits and usages of the people'. As examples of such Constitutions he quoted that of Lycurgus, the capitularies of Charlemagne, Magna Carta in England, and the Constitution of the United States. In France, however, he asserted that such periodical conventions would be productive of 'schisms, unrest and anarchy'.

He considered that in order to placate all sections of the nation, the

Assembly should recognise the right of all citizens at any time to explain 'by word of mouth, in print or by publication' their criticisms of the Constitution, subject only to the understanding that in the meantime the laws were to be obeyed. But Malouet's more serious criticism was directed against the absence of the royal participation in the constituent function. He argued that not only should the King's sanction be obtained for the Constitution as a whole, but where he considered it at any time to be contrary to the public interest and the 'general will', he should have the right to suspend it and to demand that the people manifest its express will through chosen representatives. And where the legislature refused to abide by these conditions, the King should be granted the further right of dismissing the legislature and ordering a general election. In these conclusions he was generally supported by the Right Wing deputies.

But Malouet's proposals were ridiculed as a counter-revolutionary measure by the majority of deputies, including more particularly Le Chapelier, the spokesman of the Left Centre, whilst they were strongly condemned as placing too much power in the hands of the King.

From the Left Wing there was an even greater measure of criticism, more especially directed against the failure of the Committees to implement adequately the right of the nation to modify the Constitution, at any time, of its own initiative. This, declared Robespierre, was equivalent to denying the sovereignty of the 'general will' itself. Both he and Pétion de Villeneuve demanded that a National Convention should be summoned every twenty years in order that the 'general will' of the people should find expression, and that such a Convention should be placed outside the sphere of any possible interference from the existing legislature.

D'André supported Robespierre and Pétion in claiming that no restriction should be set upon the right of the people to change its constitution, but he believed that any change should be postponed for thirty years, which alone would ensure a necessary period of tranquillity. Other deputies suggested ten or fifteen years before any change should be initiated. Desmeuniers thought ten years a sufficiently long period, but he considered that thereafter revision of details alone should be permissible. 'Suppose', he asked, 'that the majority of the nation were to demand a republic? On this hypothesis, should it not be obligatory to change the Constitution?'

Regnaud also supported Robespierre in asserting that the plan was an attack on the inherent sovereignty of the people. Even Lafayette emphasised that 'This same Assembly, which has recognised the sovereignty of the French nation, and which has recognised the right which it has to give itself a government, cannot disregard the right which it has to modify that government. . . . I believe that it would be indicative of contempt for the sovereign rights of the French people were a proposition to be adopted which would deprive them of this right for thirty years.' A similar opinion was voiced by Merlin and Chabroud, amongst other deputies.

But the Constitutional Party held firm to the principles laid down by the Joint Committees. Their plan was powerfully supported by Camus and Tronchet, as also by Le Chapelier. It was, however, Frochot, a close friend of Mirabeau, who on August 31st, 1791, submitted a revised plan, based on these same principles, which commanded universal admiration and would undoubtedly have considerably influenced final legislation on the question of the revision, had speed in completing the Constitution not prevented its full discussion.[1]

Frochot commenced by showing that the problem with which the Assembly was faced was that of guaranteeing to the people the Constitution 'as against themselves', or at least against that 'irresistible propensity of human nature to seek continually to change its position in order to attain a chimerical improvement', of guaranteeing to the people the Constitution against the attacks of rebels and the enterprises of its delegates or representatives; and finally that of giving to the sovereign people a legal means of reforming in part, or changing in its entirety, that Constitution which it had sworn to observe.

Frochot thereupon showed that there was 'an essential difference between a partial reform and a total reconstruction of the Constitution, which might escape the eye of the legislator'. The former did not necessitate the employment of the sovereign power in its entirety, whilst the latter did. 'Is the power of changing the Constitution', he asked, 'entirely inseparable from that of reforming it? When a partial reform is desired by the people, is it necessary that to the reformative power given them by their representatives should be added the terrible power of destroying at their will?'

Just as the sovereign power was regarded as delegating its purely legislative functions to the Assembly, Frochot went on to show, so it

---

[1] It caused 'une sensation profonde' and the Assembly unanimously demanded that it be printed.—Buchez et Roux, op. cit., Vol. XI, p. 372.

may give to other representatives the sovereign power of reforming the Constitution, without it being necessary for the people to alienate in any way its own sovereign power. A separation of the functions of partial reform and of complete change was, therefore, essential, otherwise the need for any small partial reform might well imperil the whole of the Constitution. It was, therefore, prudent, whilst giving the greatest possible latitude to the interpretation of the 'general will', to separate these functions, and so enable the people to confide the right of partial reform to their representatives without at the same time placing in their hands powers of destruction.

In order to solve this problem, Frochot produced a plan which (i) provided a means of partially reforming the Constitution without placing the whole of it in danger; (ii) provided a means of ascertaining the will of the people upon such reform; (iii) provided a legal means of changing the whole of the Constitution; and (iv) provided a means of ascertaining the will of the people upon such complete constitutional change.[1] Were these objects to be obtained, clearly the question of fixing any particular date for such reform did not arise, as it would be for the people to decide when such action was necessary.

Frochot thereupon cited a National Convention and a Constituent Corporation as being the organs charged with the duty of carrying out such tasks. The Convention was to consist of an assembly of representatives charged with the institution of partial reforms in the Constitution, whilst the Constituent Corporation was to be a similar assembly whose duties would be either the redistribution of the powers of government or the creation of a completely new Constitution.

'France', he exclaimed, 'has a representative government . . . the legislative body deliberates, the citizens address petitions to it; the legislative body declares the general will, the citizens express their particular wills. The act of assembling the National Convention or the Constituent Corporation is essentially an act of the general will . . . which cannot be expressed except through the representatives of the people.' But in the event of the acts of the legislature not entirely reflecting the 'general will', there arose the necessity of the royal sanction, but this latter was not to apply to the act of convocation itself, for this emanated from the essential sovereignty of the people, and therefore was an act of the supreme power. But as the royal sanction did not apply, what precaution was to be taken against the possibility of the people themselves being mistaken? Clearly, by

---

[1] Cf. Appendix for full details of Frochot's scheme.

providing that two further legislatures, freely elected, should each be empowered to carry through the reforms or changes considered desirable as the case might be. There could be no doubt about the 'general will', and the National Convention or Constituent Corporation could be assembled with confidence.

Frochot's scheme was supported by Beaumetz, who emphasised that, 'whilst we regard it as a solemn duty on the part of the National Assembly to declare solemnly the right of the nation, every day and every hour, to change the Constitution in its entirety, we are, at the same time, persuaded that the active exercise of this right would be contrary to its interests'. Thouret was more critical. 'What is essential to the nation,' he declared, 'which enjoys a fundamentally good Constitution, is the power of rectifying its faults in detail. It is not then essential to provide for the event of a total overthrow of a Constitution founded on the unchanging basis of justice and the eternal principles of reason.'

But as Frochot's scheme protected the interests of the Third Estate in two ways, by making complete change dependent upon the sanction of a Constituent Corporation, elected partly according to taxable capacity, and by making the final arbiter in any such decision the legislature itself, it received an enthusiastic reception from the majority of the deputies in the Assembly.

Thus after further argument and protest, Titre VII of the Constitution was finally drawn up, which laid down the following procedure. After three consecutive legislatures had all requested the alteration of an Article in the Constitution, the revision would be carried out. The fourth legislature would then, after being augmented by two hundred and forty-nine additional deputies elected in each *département* by doubling the ordinary number furnished on the basis of its population, form the Revisional Convention, meeting as one chamber. No member of the third legislature, which had demanded the change, could be elected to this Convention. After taking the prescribed oaths, the Convention would then proceed to sanction the revision or modify it if necessary, and then the specially elected additional representatives were to retire to their constituencies and take no further part in legislation.

The two legislative assemblies which were to follow the Constituent Assembly of 1789–91 were, it may be noted, deprived of this right of demanding reform.

The attitude of the Assembly to the revision of the Constitution was severely criticised by Fonteneau.[1] 'This system was not a good one,' he writes. 'By the addition to the titular representatives of two hundred and forty-nine ephemeral representatives, the Revisional Convention, if indeed it ever became one, would only have the appearance of a Constituent Assembly.   For the two hundred and forty-nine temporary deputies would find themselves in an inferior situation to the deputies destined to form the legislative body, and consequently, without influence on the decision to be taken.'

Clermont-Tonnerre was equally sceptical.   'When this demand had been repeated three times by as many legislatures of the same mind and the same interest, a fourth also having the same mind and the same interest would become the Revisional Convention.   To it would be joined two hundred and forty-nine members, an impotent minority, even supposing them to be opposed to the desires revealed by the permanent members.'

But, in effect, the Assembly had succeeded in making the bourgeois citadel virtually inviolate.   They believed that the sovereign power of the 'general will' was sufficiently provided for by the system of Revisional Conventions.   Even Salles appeared to be convinced, although he did demand the establishment of a more direct channel by which this will could be made effective.[2]

The Assembly had thus, in short, repeated the method which it had adopted to justify the creation of an independent legislative will.   It had identified its policy with the current *mystique* by recognising that the nation as a whole held the substance of the sovereign power.   But it had perforce to delegate this power—so far as the initiative for revision was concerned, to the legislative body, and so far as the revision itself was concerned, to a specially elected convention.   In this way, it was asserted, changes could be made in the Constitution without upsetting the life of the State.   The people participated in this power, but only as a spectator.   It was not to interfere in the work of revision, but it always had the knowledge that it could do so.   Frochot and Barnave, in particular, appear to have believed that popular

[1] *Du Pouvoir Constituant en France*, p. 50.

[2] He asserted that whilst the primary assemblies of the country reflected the general will, the constituent convention made up of representatives elected from these assemblies should itself be essentially constituent, and thus invested with the plenitude of sovereignty.   On the other hand, whilst the legislature was to have the right to decide whether or not the changes advocated by the primary bodies were to be effected, a negative decision of two successive legislatures was to be over-ruled where the nation persisted in demanding such changes, and a third legislature should therefore be compelled to summon a national convention.

sovereignty was thus reconciled in the only conceivable way with the representative principle of government, which had at the same time been so formulated as best to preserve bourgeois supremacy.

But Robespierre, a little shrewder, foresaw that when the will of the people did succeed in making itself heard, it would be a further call to revolution.

For the decision of the Assembly to reinstate the King had been widely interpreted as proving the royalist sympathies of the deputies. The Assembly thus shared in the suspicion and hatred with which the King was now universally regarded. And the Constitution, being identified with the Assembly, was destined scarcely to outlast it. As one historian has recently written: 'The alliance of the middle and lower classes against tyranny and privilege may have been a *mariage de convenance* rather than a love match. It did not long survive their common victory.' To the masses, the policy of the Assembly appeared to be little more than that of arresting the Revolution, and, by a repression of a wider democratic liberty, establishing a bourgeois plutocracy.

The Constitution of 1791 was intended to last for ten years without revision. The Assembly would have been astounded had they known that, despite their precautions, within that period of time a fourth Constitution was to reach the Statute Book.

CHAPTER VIII

CHURCH AND STATE

IN formulating a new Constitution for their country in terms of the
sovereignty of the 'general will' of the people, the deputies of the
National Assembly had been confronted with purely political problems
which had not proved to be, in practice, insuperable. But when the
Assembly turned to ecclesiastical questions, a difficult situation arose.
For it was confronted by a second sovereign power, that of the Pope,
supreme in all spiritual matters and possessed of no small additional
authority and power at a more materialistic level. It had been found
possible to constitutionalise the King. To constitutionalise the Pope
in so far as his relations with the new France were concerned was to
prove an even more difficult matter. How was the liberal outlook of
a constitutional democracy to be reconciled with the reactionary viewpoint of an absolute Papacy?

That reform of the Church was a vital necessity had been recognised
by all classes, both within and without the Church. It had been
demanded by the *cahiers* of all three Orders;[1] it was regarded as long
overdue by many of the higher clergy, as also by the rank and file of
the lower clergy. The latter were particularly dissatisfied with the
existing régime in that all avenues of promotion were largely closed to
them. Originally, the King had selected the candidates for bishoprics
and they, in turn, had chosen the clergy. The Pope had consecrated
the men upon whom the King's choice had fallen, and through the
bishops had ordained the clergy. Thus as landowners and recipients
of ecclesiastical revenues, the clergy had been subject to the King. In
matters spiritual, they owed allegiance to the Pope. The system had
not worked badly so long as selection for high office had been based on
merit. But during the eighteenth century, and more particularly
from 1750 onwards, the higher offices in the Church had gone to men
of birth and wealth rather than to men of piety and learning, and a new
episcopal aristocracy had been created to which the humbler clergy

---

[1] Cf. Chassin, C. L.: *Les Cahiers des Curés* (1882); Champion: *La Séparation de
l'Eglise et de l'Etat en 1794* (1903), esp. Chap. VI, p. 58; also Mathiez, A.: *Rome et
le Clergé Français sous la Constituante*, pp. 20 f.

had no hope of aspiring. Indeed, the King had so far alienated his interest in the matter that the appointment of bishops had fallen largely into the hands of a royal official, charged with the administration of the *feuille des bénéfices*.

Having identified the sovereign power in the State with the 'general will' of the nation, it seemed logical to the majority of deputies in the Assembly that the nation should fall heir to all powers which had previously been vested in the King. Thus it appeared that the Assembly, as representative of the sovereign nation, should take over the functions which had been a prerogative of the King. In 1789, there were no very clear ideas amongst the deputies as to what was entailed by such a departure from pre-existing tradition. Later, distinct cleavages of opinion were to arise in the Assembly, more particularly between the Monarchist and Right Wing elements and the more progressive Constitutionalists who had the general support of the ultras of the extreme Left Wing.

Despite the widespread demand for reform at the outbreak of the Revolution, however, there was little evidence of any weakening in the loyalty of the nation as a whole to the Catholic faith. The parish priest remained the most important official in the community, the servant of a Church whose spiritual dictatorship had been of greater significance in the life of the average man than the tyranny which had been exercised by the temporal power. Again, it was the parish priest, rather than the bishop or archbishop, who controlled the loyalty of the masses. The humbler clergy, divorced socially as well as sympathetically from the hierarchy of higher officials, had thus become a force to be reckoned with. That they had identified themselves with the Third Estate, and had played so important a part in bringing about the establishment of the National Assembly itself, was one of the most significant facts of the Revolution.

The Assembly, therefore, out of gratitude to the humbler clergy, and at the same time fully cognisant of their power in the State, were loath to do anything which might strain their loyalty or prove a source of embarrassment to them. It had, therefore, not failed to pay homage to the Catholic faith where opportunity served. Thus the inauguration of the Assembly itself had been consecrated by a religious procession and the celebration of High Mass. To Target, this day appeared as one which Providence seemed to desire to solemnise by 'converting the temple of religion into the temple of the fatherland'. And during the debates leading up to the codification of the Declaration of Rights, serious efforts had been made to reconcile the principles of religion with the tenets of the current *mystique*. 'What is nature?' asked the Comte de Virieu. 'Is it not a word empty of meaning, leading us to consider material things alone, if it hides from us the image of the Creator?' 'In speaking of nature, should not one speak of its Creator?' demanded Lally-Tollendal. To the Bishop of Clermont, religion was 'the eternal reason which watched over the scheme of things'. It was the Supreme Being who had made men free and equal in rights, according to the Abbé Bonnefoi, whilst it was the 'author of nature', asserted the Bishop of Langres, that had placed in all men the desire for liberty and happiness and the means of attaining them.

The expression of similar sentiments by other deputies eventually led to the decision of the Assembly to preface the Declaration itself by an invocation of the Supreme Being. As the Archbishop of Aix said, 'Religion is the seal of a Declaration which assures to man his rights and his liberty.' Thus, despite an ironical suggestion from the Vicomte de Mirabeau that it might be wise to place the Decalogue in its entirety at the head of the Declaration, the deputies included the following dedication in the preamble thereto: 'The National Assembly recognises and declares, in the presence of, and under the auspices of, the Supreme Being, the following rights of man and of the citizen.'

But did such rights include that of religious freedom? Here the Assembly was placed in a dilemma. For the principle of the sovereignty of the nation had been decreed in such terms that the sovereign power was held to reside in the 'general will' of the people— all of the people—and the people included many non-Catholics.[1] Many of the deputies themselves were not Catholics. It was therefore difficult to discriminate against bearers of the sovereign power on religious grounds. In the Assembly, there was much discussion about this question, which included a vehement appeal by Rabaut de St. Etienne on behalf of his constituency, which included some 120,000 Protestants, that the edict of November, 1787, should be fully implemented. This edict granted liberty of conscience to the Protestants, but not full liberty of worship. After much discussion, the Assembly ultimately got out of the difficulty by decreeing toleration of

[1] The census of 1802 gave the number of Protestants as 479,312 (Aulard: *Christianity and the French Revolution*, p. 24). In 1789 there were also many Jews settled chiefly in the south-west and east of France, and in Paris itself (Aulard, op. cit., p. 23).

all religions, but it did not dare to alienate the members of the clergy by fully supporting the pleas of many deputies, particularly those of the Left Wing, for full religious freedom. 'No one shall be penalised for his opinions, even religious ones,' ran the decree, 'provided that they do not lead to a disturbance of the public order established by the law.' The insertion of the word 'even' is an indication that religious toleration was regarded as a greater concession than any of the other freedoms which had been incorporated in the Declaration.

For similar reasons it was not possible for the Assembly to declare the Catholic faith to be the official religion of the state. The question did not directly arise until April 12th, 1790, when Dom Gerle asked the deputies to decree that 'the Catholic, Apostolic and Roman religion should be, and should always remain, the religion of the nation, and that its worship should be the only public and authorised one'. The Assembly requested an adjournment, and on the following day countered Dom Gerle's motion with the following decree, proposed by La Rochefoucauld: 'The National Assembly, considering that it neither has, nor can have, any power over conscience or over religious opinion, and that the majesty of religion and the profound respect due to it alike forbid it becoming the subject of discussion; considering that the attachment of the Assembly to the Catholic, Apostolic and Roman religion cannot be called in question at a time when the expenses of this religion are being given primary consideration in the national budget, and when, with a unanimous sentiment of respect, it has expressed its feelings in the only way befitting the dignity of religion and the character of the National Assembly, decrees that it cannot and ought not to deliberate on the motion proposed.' It is noteworthy that, although the decree was passed, nearly three hundred deputies voted against it and therefore impliably in favour of that of Dom Gerle.[1]

On the evening of August 4th, 1789, there had been no opposition to the *arrêtés* which affected the wealth and revenue of the Church. Article V abolished all tithes and substitutes for tithes, but permitted their provisional collection until the Assembly could decide upon 'some other means of providing for the expenses of Divine worship, for the

---

[1] The voting is given by the *Moniteur* as follows:

For			*Against*		
Clergy	.	156	Clergy	.	144
Nobles	.	196	Nobles	.	104
Commons	.	551	Commons	.	49
		903			297

sustenance of the ministers of the altar, the relief of the poor, and the repair and reconstruction of churches and presbyteries'. Article VIII suppressed the occasional fees of county priests, but not until their stipends had been increased and their pensions provided for. Article XII abolished the *annates*, an annual payment of some three million francs to the Pope, whilst Article XIV forbade the holding of plural benefices where their joint value amounted to more than three thousand francs annually.

It is true that, in the days which followed, some criticism was levelled against particular aspects of the legislation of August 4th. One *curé* asked, 'When you invited us, in the name of the God of Peace, to join you, it was, then, that you might cut our throats the more easily.' Several other deputies spoke in similar vein. But they were indignantly repudiated by the mass of the clergy. The Bishop of Dijon emphasised that 'the clergy would know how to make any sacrifices which might be asked for'. The Bishop of Langres asked the Assembly 'not to attribute to the whole Order the individual views of certain of its members', whilst the Archbishop of Paris announced gravely, 'Gentlemen, in the name of my brethren, in the name of my co-operators, in that of all members of the clergy in this august Assembly, and in my own name, we place the whole of the titles of the Church in the hands of a just and generous nation.' For Grégoire, by whom their abolition had been proposed, the *annates* were 'a monument of simony which had already been condemned by the Council of Bâle'.

Perhaps this lack of opposition to the decrees of August 4th was in the nature of a lull before the storm. The abolition of the *annates* represented the first rupture of the Concordat of 1516. And yet few voices were raised in opposition. The *arrêtés* were the first attack made by the Assembly on the ecclesiastical revenues, but even those prelates who were later to become the centre of Right Wing opposition to the Civil Constitution were silent, possibly because they did not as yet realise the extent of the demands which were so soon to be made upon the Church.

And by the end of October, it was becoming clear to the majority of deputies in the Assembly that such demands could not long be delayed. Not only were the taxes not being collected, but the market for loans had been virtually exhausted, whilst the normal progress of trade and industry had suffered severely from the uncertainties arising out of the events of the previous six months. The position was becoming desperate, and the eyes of the Assembly inevitably turned towards the immense wealth of the Church, estimated by Rabaut de St. Etienne to be of the value of one-fifth of the land in the country.[1] How could the appropriation of this wealth be justified?

The answer clearly lay in terms of the sovereignty of the 'general will' of the nation. Such a will was omnipotent, and no partial will, such as that of an ecclesiastical corporation, could stand against it. This argument was put most clearly by Thouret, supporting the views of the Constitutionalists. 'The law can pronounce', he said, 'that any corporation is no longer a proprietor just as it may have previously pronounced it to be so; this is why the destruction of such a body is not a murder; hence, the act by which the National Assembly annihilates the property right which supposedly inheres in the clergy is in no way a spoliation. It is only necessary to declare that such corporations can no longer hold property. . . . The clergy have already ceased to be a political body; it is therefore merely for the law to declare that they are no longer a property-owning body. So far as the wealth of the Church is concerned, the nation has the right to recover it, as it has permitted the Church to hold it, but only in trust for the nation.'

In point of fact, the appropriation of the wealth of the Church had been forecast as early as August 6th, when Buzot, answering the objections of several prelates to the decrees of August 4th, had asserted that 'The clergy can do no better than save appearances by gracefully accepting those sacrifices which the force of circumstances compels them to make. . . . There can be no doubt that the wealth of the Church belongs to the nation.' The matter had not been then pursued, but by the end of October it was apparent that the attitude of the Right Wing was hardening towards the policy of the Constitutionalists and the Left. Thouret's statement was made in answer to an eloquent speech of the Abbé Maury claiming that the wealth of the Church was sacred and could not be touched by the Assembly. Maury was strongly supported by Boisgelin, the Archbishop of Aix, who took a rather different line in asserting that the Church was not the proprietor of its wealth, but merely a trustee and that it would betray its trust in handing over this wealth to the nation. Even Camus, the Jansenist, gave it as his opinion that the Clergy were the sole proprietors of the wealth of the Church because they had received from the King the right both to acquire and to dispose of it. He

---

[1] In terms of income, Talleyrand estimated it to yield an annual revenue of 150 million livres, Treilhard 200 million livres and Chasset 303 million livres.

opposed Treilhard's demand for its appropriation on the grounds outlined by Thouret, by insisting that the whole ecclesiastical position should be reviewed, and a Civil Constitution of the Clergy drawn up before the question of the disposal of this wealth should be decided. This did not mean that Camus, a member of the Constitutional Group, had failed to identify himself with its policy. In May, 1790, he could assert that 'The Church is within the State, the State is not within the Church,' and as we shall find later he was one of the strongest supporters of the absolute sovereignty of the nation. His opposition to Treilhard was based on a matter of legal procedure at this stage.

The argument of the Left Centre was reinforced by a brilliant speech from Barnave, who asserted that there were two possibilities only. Either the nation had provided the Church with its wealth over the centuries in order that it could fulfil certain functions in the State, in which case the provision by the State of the means to carry on such functions meant that the nation could repossess itself of its inheritance.

Alternatively, the funds of the Church had merely been placed in its trust to secure the provision of such services. In this case, the Church had never been proprietor of this wealth. Hence, he emphasised, 'The fundamental right of the nation, the situation in which the State finds itself, the indispensable necessity of providing adequately for the great mass of the clergy themselves, all these factors compel you to recognise that the nation is the true proprietor of that wealth which has, up to the present time, been enjoyed by the Church.'

The arguments for and against the taking over by the State of the property of the Church lasted almost for one month, but ultimately it was clear that the majority, of the deputies, including many of the Clergy, were in favour of this step. But anxious not to lose the support of the mass of the clergy, the Constitutionalists did not go so far as to commit themselves on the vexed problem of ownership, but compromised by decreeing that 'The wealth of the Church is at the disposal of the nation,' a somewhat vague phrase[1] which did not,

---

[1] That this decree was not regarded as implying confiscation is confirmed by a statement made by Chasset on April 9th, 1790, when he referred to the decree of November 2nd as 'rien, tant que le clergé n'était pas exproprié' (*Mon.*, Vol. IV, p. 84). Boisgelin was less sanguine. On November 3rd he wrote, 'La cause du clergé est perdue . . . j'ai pourtant gagné trois points: (1) on n'a pas dit que la propriété appartient à la nation, on a dit seulement que les biens étaient à sa disposition. . . .' (Arch. Nat. M. 788, quoted Mathiez, op. cit., p. 85).

however, prevent it from ordering the sale of some 400 million livres' worth of Church and Crown property on the following December 19th. The clergy had been further placated by a promise that no living should be of a less annual value than 1,200 francs, together with a house and garden, and that the State would provide in a fitting manner for the expenses of public worship and for the relief of the poor.

It is noteworthy that the influence of the mob was almost as decisive during this debate as it had been during the debates on the veto. The dissenting clergy were abused and threatened; the Abbé Maury on one occasion was pursued by the mob and saved his life only by taking refuge in a house in the Rue Sainte-Anne.[1]

As a logical outcome of the nationalisation of the wealth of the Church, the abolition of monastic vows and the suppression of monasteries and convents was decreed on February 13th, 1790.[2] Such institutions could no longer survive once their means of existence had been appropriated by the State. Pensions were provided for the regular clergy and nuns thus thrown upon the world.

But behind the policy of the Constitutionalists and the extreme Left Wing there lay a deeper motive for reform of the Church than that of a mere confiscation of its wealth with a view to easing a financial crisis. To ensure the success of the Revolution and to consolidate the position of the Third Estate, it appeared necessary to secure the allegiance of the clergy to the new régime. Much of the power of the Church had been removed by the nationalisation of its wealth. But in addition, it was vital to purge it of all reactionary elements by securing the preferment of men who would be loyal to the existing order. There existed a constant fear that the Pope, as a centre of reaction, might, by securing the support of those foreign powers who already feared the repercussion of events in France within their own territories, seek to intervene by force in the affairs of the nation.

Thus far, the Pope had been held in check by the Assembly's use of the troubles which had been fomented in Avignon and in the Comtat Venaissin, as a bargaining counter. The deputies were quite prepared, despite the protests of Bouche and certain other deputies of

---

[1] For an account of the public disturbances which took place during the debates, cf. Ludovic Sciout: *Histoire de la Constitution Civile du Clergé*.

[2] Certain exceptions were made in the case of institutions performing particularly valuable social work.

the extreme Left, to deny to these papal territories the very liberties which they had won for themselves, in order to strengthen the possibility of Papal approval, or at least to postpone the effects of Papal disapproval, of their programme of Church reform.

There equally existed a possibility that by appealing to those of the clergy whose spiritual allegiance to Rome was stronger than their temporal allegiance to Paris, the Pope might attempt to incite disaffection in the country itself by playing on the religious feeling of the people, particularly in the North and West of the country, and thus sow the seeds of counter-revolution. For either reason, it was vital to remove from positions of influence all doubtful elements within the Church.

The method by which ecclesiastical reform could be brought about lay close at hand. As in the administrative field, so in the field of church affairs, a two-fold system of reform could be introduced. Primarily, in view of the fact that the clergy had now become salaried servants of the State, it was possible to insist that all offices in the Church should be filled by popular election. The *feuille des bénéfices* previously held by the King or his nominee would thus pass to the new sovereign—the people. And secondly, on the model of the new administrative units which were to prove so useful an instrument in the dissolving of old loyalties and the checking of old corruptions, new dioceses and parishes could be created on the same geometrical pattern. By destroying the parochial pattern of *l'ancien régime*, there would be a tendency to uproot old ties between Church and people, which would hinder the possible growth of centres of reaction.

The Constitutionalists felt that in carrying out this programme they could count to no small extent on the pronounced gallicanism of many of the clergy, on their revolutionary sentiment, as also on the ambitions of many priests who now saw possibilities of preferment for the first time. Further, the improved stipends of the clergy would be conducive to loyalty. Thus armed, the Left Centre turned to the Ecclesiastical Committee, which, established by the Assembly on August 20th, 1789, had so far made little progress.[1]

This Committee, on which the members of the Left Centre were

---

[1] Its members were as follows: The Bishops of Clermont and Luçon, the Prince de Robecq and the Marquis de Bouthillier, the Abbé Vaneau and the Abbé Grandin, as also the curé de La Lande, who were opposed to the Civil Constitution; Lanjuinais, d'Ormesson, Sallé de Choux, Legrand and Durand de Maillane, who were lukewarm supporters of the Constitution; Treilhard, Despatis de Courteilles and Martineau, who alone advocated the policy of the Left Centre.

in a minority, had failed to make progress largely because of the conflicting political views of its members. Thus far it had done little but half-heartedly attempt an inventory of Church wealth. The Committee had elected as its President the Bishop of Clermont, but he had resigned following the Assembly's decree of November 2nd. One member alone had attempted to get something done—Durand de Maillane. On November 3rd he had submitted a scheme to the Committee which he believed would reconcile the rights of the King, the Church and the people. His plan, whilst condemning the Concordat, sought to perpetuate good relations with the Papacy by permitting all newly elected Bishops to send *une profession de foi* to the Pope as a proof of their attachment and loyalty to the Church of Rome. Three candidates, in the event of a vacancy, were to be chosen by an assembly composed of the Chapter of the vacant diocese, the two nearest bishops, and a certain number of the members of the directory of the *département*. The assembly was to meet under the presidency of the Metropolitan or of another bishop designated by him. From this panel of three, the King would choose the successful candidate. In turn, the bishops would choose the clergy. Despite the moderation of Durand's plan, however, it was shelved following the opposition of the two Bishops on the Committee.

The Ecclesiastical Committee was in this moribund state when the Left Centre Group decided to take action. 'The Ecclesiastical Committee has been so badly composed', wrote Thomas Lindet, 'that it is difficult for it to do any useful work. It is necessary to reorganise it.' Impatient at the delay, the Constitutionalists succeeded in securing, on February 7th, 1790, the appointment of an additional fifteen members to the Committee, all members of the Left Wing.[1] As Durand de Maillane remarked, 'The Jacobins now have a predominating influence in the Committee.'[2] As a result, nine of the original members of the Committee resigned, thus considerably reducing Right Wing opposition.

Nevertheless, the moderates on the Committee were not prepared to accept the views of the newly elected members. Led by Lanjuinais, they could have proved a source of embarrassment to the Left Centre deputies had the Right Wing representatives who remained

[1] The new members were: Dom Gerle, Dionis du Séjour, the Abbé de Montesquiou, Guillaume, de la Coste, Dupont de Nemours, Massieu, the Abbé Expilly, Chasset, the Abbé Gassendi, Boislandry, Defermont, Dom Breton, La Poule and Thibault.

[2] *Histoire apologétique du Comité ecclésiastique*, quoted Mathiez, op. cit., p. 99.

joined with them. This, however, they refused to do, and the re-constituted Committee therefore lost little time in getting down to the work of reform. It divided itself into three sub-committees, the first to deal with the Civil Constitution of the Clergy and the administration of the Church finances, the second to prepare schemes for the sale of Church property and the third to conduct the day-to-day business of the Committee and deal with *mémoires* received in connection with its work. On May 29th, the first sub-committee, which included the lawyer Martineau, the Abbé Expilly and Durand de Maillane, laid its first draft of the new Constitution before the Assembly. The day was well chosen, as the King, acting upon Bailly's advice to make himself more popular with the masses, had just declared his solidarity with the Assembly, had condemned all opposition to its decrees, and had prohibited the wearing of any favour other than the tricolour.

The Committee's plan was yet relatively conservative. Martineau, its *rapporteur*, prefaced his remarks by insisting that the question before the Assembly was primarily one of restoring to religion its energy and its dignity. 'Institutions', he declared, 'must be founded on the sacred basis of religion, on faith in the Supreme Being, the sovereign dispenser of good and ill, the avenger of crime and the source of virtue. . . . It is to religion above all, gentlemen, that you have bound the success of your labours. Kings, subjects, magistrates—civil and military—you have required from them all the solemn oath of fidelity to the nation, the law and the King, and that they should maintain with all their power the Constitution you have established. What have you accomplished by this? You have proclaimed aloud to all that the salvation of the Empire is closely bound up with religion. For without religion, an oath is but an empty word.'

Martineau then proceeded to reinforce this bid for the sympathy of the clergy by insisting at some length that the proposed reforms he was about to lay before the Assembly would bring about no more than a return to the discipline and organisation of the early Church.

After completing these introductory remarks, Martineau then turned to the main proposals of the Committee, which were to occupy the Assembly in heated debate for some six weeks. Primarily, the Committee proposed that the officials of the Church—the word was significant—were to be elected by the people. 'If the bishops, the *curés* and other ministers of religion are established for the benefit of the people, what can be more reasonable than that the people should choose them?' asked Martineau. As the sovereign power in the State, the people had inherited the rights which had been previously held by the King, the seigneurs and by the other bodies which had been concerned with the election of Church officials. But, in order to placate the clergy, the Committee had decided that only ordained ministers of the Church were to be eligible for election, and that a service qualification should be introduced, varying in length according to the importance of the position to be filled. Further, it was proposed that each successful candidate, before receiving canonical institution, should be examined as to his doctrine and beliefs, the *curés* by the bishop, the bishop by his Metropolitan, and the Metropolitan himself by the senior bishops.

Secondly, considerable administrative reforms were to be instituted in the organisation of the Church. The older dioceses were to be remoulded along the lines of the new *départements* which characterised the new civil administration, whilst the number of parishes in each diocese were to be reorganised with a view to equalising the numbers of inhabitants in each parish. And finally, so far as the payment of the clergy was concerned, a graduated scale was to be introduced, which would reassess and fix all salaries from that of the Archbishop of Paris down to that of the humblest *curé*.

Other administrative details followed. The principle of the sovereignty of the nation was firmly laid down. The organisation and administration of the Church, its finances and its personnel were to become a Department of State. Only in the spiritual sphere was allegiance to Rome to be tolerated.[1]

As may be expected, considerable opposition to such a principle was immediately forthcoming, not only from the Right Wing Groups and the reactionary prelates, but also from many of the clergy who up to this point had been wholehearted supporters of the Revolution. Such an unwarrantable interference with matters which were, to them, strictly a concern of the Church alone, strained their loyalty to breaking-point. The Archbishop of Aix led the opposition of the higher Clergy. The Church, he claimed, was established by the apostles; no earthly power had the right to interfere with it. Hence no changes could be made in the organisation of the Church without the concurrence of an ecclesiastical commission. He was supported by the Bishop of Lydda, who argued emphatically that the nation had not the power to interfere with spiritual matters nor with the adminis-

[1] Cf. Mathiez: *Rome et le Clergé Français sous la Constituante*, pp. 158 f.

tration of Church affairs.   The same point was urged by many other
speakers, some of whom also criticised, in lengthy historical arguments, the accuracy of Martineau's statement that such reforms
reflected the spirit and organisation of the primitive Church.

But the Constitutionalists, supported by the extreme Left Wing,
remained adamant.   They could tolerate no limitation of the power of
the sovereign people.   'When the sovereign power believes a reform
to be necessary,' said Treilhard, 'nothing can oppose it.   The State
may recognise, or refuse to recognise, a religion; it can, in its absolute
discretion, declare that such and such an established religion shall
exist in this place or that, under such and such conditions.   The right
of the sovereign power is entirely independent of any particular faith
or dogma.'   Camus further emphasised this position.   'Ministers of
the Church within a State may say that they must have bishops in the
principal towns, *curés* in the smaller ones.   The civil power says to
them, "Here are the cities.   Set up your bishops.   Here are the
towns.   Establish your clergy . . ."   We are a national convention,'
he concluded.   'We have assuredly the power to change a religion
itself, but we do not desire to do so.'

But both Treilhard and Camus, together with several other
members of the Left Centre Group, including Goupil de Préfeln,
Martineau, Garat and Reubell, were prepared to adopt a more con-
ciliatory attitude than the majority of Left Wing deputies.   In
particular they were willing to negotiate along the lines of a compromise solution put forward by the Abbé Jacquemard and a *curé*
de Gouttes.

Jacquemard's argument was that whilst the choice of bishops must
remain a matter for the Church, their election resting in the hands
of an Electoral College, the diocesan synod composing the College
should be enlarged by the addition of members of the administrative
assembly of the *département* concerned.   De Gouttes took this proposal further and attempted to reconcile Jacquemard's argument with
the principle that the nation alone was the sovereign power.   Undoubtedly the people had the indisputable right, ingeniously argued
de Gouttes, to elect its officials, whether civil or ecclesiastical.   But,
owing to the size of the nation, it was not possible for the people to
elect these officials directly, but only through representatives.   The
question therefore arose, which representatives were most suited for
this purpose?   To quote de Goutte's own words, 'If the people itself
can take part in any particular election, the question is not in doubt.

But where the people is too numerous to take part directly, it can do so only through delegates. The only question, therefore, to be solved is how to determine the method of choosing the most suitable delegates for this purpose.' Clearly, a joint assembly of the diocesan synod and the civil administrative officials, of the type envisaged by Jacquemard, was the ideal electoral body.

But such a plan encountered violent opposition from the more extreme deputies of the Left Wing. Robespierre attacked it as threatening the very heart of the doctrine of popular sovereignty. 'The right of electing', he insisted, 'cannot belong to an administrative body; it can belong to the sovereign power alone, and this right can be exercised only by the citizens or by their direct representatives. . . . You propose, however, to summon them to exercise this right, not as citizens, but as members of the Clergy, as members of a particular body. Hence you are violating a fundamental principle. Not only are you breaking the principle of equality of political right; you are making of the clergy an isolated body. . . . When you say that such a principle violates the spirit of piety, that it is contrary to the requirements of common sense, that the people are too corrupt to be trusted with such elections, do you not see that this would be equally true of every kind of election? The clergy are no purer than the mass of the people.' Robespierre was anxious not only to abolish all archbishops and cardinals, but also to permit popularly elected bishops and clergy to marry should they so desire.[1] He was supported, with slight modifications in this argument, by Fréteau and by Roederer, amongst other deputies.

Many of the members of the Left Centre, however, opposed Jacquemard's compromise proposal for rather different reasons. They argued that it was contrary to the principle of the separation of the powers of government which had already been accepted by the Assembly. This argument was put most clearly by Le Chapelier. 'The division of powers', he insisted, 'as a doctrine is opposed to the establishment of any partial corporation in the State. This, indeed, would destroy the doctrine itself. Administrative assemblies cannot be electoral bodies, and the perpetuation of this confusion will result in the destruction of the fundamental laws of the constitution. You

---

[1] It is interesting to note that the marriage of priests had considerable popular support. Mirabeau, indeed, accused Robespierre of stealing his motion on this subject. Cf. Mathiez: *Rome et le Clergé Français sous la Constituante*, p. 167, and the pamphlets there cited in Footnote (i).

will establish new corporations in the place of those which you have destroyed. . . . Who has the greatest interest in ensuring a wise choice of clergymen? Is it not essentially the people rather than the ministers of the Church? Is a consecrated priest necessary for this task? No, without doubt.'

This argument was reinforced by Barnave. 'Apart from the basic principles written into our constitution', he asserted, 'there is a further political aspect of this matter. The powers of Government can be delegated in one of two ways only, either by the people, or by those who have directly received from them the power to act on their behalf. The great danger which you have to avoid is the splitting-up of power amongst different bodies of varying degrees of importance. Nothing can be more opposed to the principles of a good constitution than the grant to any particular body of the power to regenerate itself. . . . The people, in exercising its right to elect, can in no way interfere with the spiritual affairs of the Church.'

Other deputies, including Mirabeau and Biauzat, also identified themselves with this point of view. Thus the debate continued. The dissenting clergy and the more reactionary deputies brought forward an inconceivable number of historical arguments to prove that the bishops, as successors of the Apostles, had always been elected and instituted by the Church alone. Equally, historical arguments intended to prove that in the days of the primitive Church the bishops and clergy had been elected by the people, interspersed with further arguments invoking the will of the sovereign people and the doctrine of the separation of powers, were used to oppose them. One of the final speeches was made by a Left Wing *curé*, who concluded by saying, 'Thus the law is made for all; the will of all is necessary to establish discipline. . . . I conclude that matters of external discipline are within the competence of the nation, which therefore has the power to determine the number and extent of dioceses and parishes.'

Some discussion had earlier arisen out of Grégoire's proposal that in no event should non-Catholics participate in the election of Church officials. This proposal brought to the fore the same difficulties which had confronted the Assembly over the question of whether or not to declare the Catholic religion to be the official religion of the State. As in that case, so in the case of the election of Church officers, it was vital to the Constitutionalists to maintain the principle of popular sovereignty, involving the will of every citizen. Hence Grégoire's motion was rejected, despite an ingenious suggestion from

Goupil de Préfeln which was designed to avoid the difficulty. He had suggested that members of the electoral assemblies who were non-Catholics should delegate their powers to an equal number of Catholics who were members of the district assemblies, authorising them to vote in their place.

Another argument which took place further underlines the importance placed by the Constitutionalists upon the maintenance intact of the doctrine of the sovereignty of the people. In the original draft of the Civil Constitution presented by Martineau, a clause had been inserted with a view to placating the Pope and the dissentient clergy, which read as follows—'The King will be petitioned to take all measures which are judged necessary to ensure the full and entire execution of the present decree.' The intention was to secure papal approval for the Bill by means of royal intervention on its behalf.

The clause was vigorously opposed by the Left Wing generally, who insisted that to accept such a proposal would be tantamount to admitting that the Assembly had not of itself sufficient power to reform the Church and its discipline, which in turn cast doubt upon its sovereignty. As Durand himself remarked, 'The bishops would be enabled, under the imposing cloak of religion, to condemn afresh all our principles of liberty and national sovereignty.'

On July 12th, 1790, a much amended version of the Civil Constitution passed into law. The first part of the Bill dealt with the re-arrangement of dioceses and parishes. The dioceses were to correspond with the new *départements*. The new parishes were to contain not more than six thousand inhabitants. The second part of the Constitution laid down the method of electing the bishops and clergy. They were to be elected in the same way as departmental and district officials respectively. The cathedral church itself was to return to its ancient status as *une église cathédrale*, whose *curé* was to be the bishop. In this way, the bishop would remain in closer contact with his flock. The third part of the Act dealt with stipends, which ranged from 50,000 livres annually for the Bishop of Paris down to 700 livres for a country *vicaire*. Finally, the fourth part established the rule that neither bishops nor clergy could absent themselves from their dioceses or parishes for more than a fortnight at any one time without obtaining special leave, and they were further debarred from holding any secular office which might interfere with their official duties. The departmental assemblies were further given power to punish church officers disobeying these regulations by depriving them of their stipends or their posts. In this way the Church was placed under the disciplinary control of the sovereign people, or rather, of the active citizens who represented them.

In general, there can be no doubt that the great majority of deputies in the Assembly, as also the greater part of the clergy, supported the Civil Constitution. Who could doubt the sovereign people had rights equal to those which had been exercised by the Kings of France over Church affairs since the sixteenth century? But, nevertheless, the existence of numbers of clergy who dissented from the provisions of the Civil Constitution could not be ignored. And the Assembly could not tolerate their presence in what had now become a service of the State. Loyalty to the Revolution, to the new Constitution of the country and to the established doctrine of the sovereignty of the people was to be insisted upon at all costs. No potential centres of opposition to the régime established by the Third Estate could be permitted; no possible focus of anti-revolutionary sentiment allowed.

Hence, on November 27th, 1790, the Constitutionalists decided to apply the test of the oath, provision for which had already been made in the Civil Constitution. In reaching this decision, the Assembly had been influenced partly by the gradual unveiling of papal hostility, which was now becoming apparent, and which had led to the first steps being taken to annex Avignon on October 27th, and partly by the growing restlessness and impatience of the mob at the continued dissension in clerical circles. The form of the oath, which was drawn up on December 24th, 1790, was as follows. 'I swear to watch carefully over the faithful placed in my charge. I swear to be faithful to the nation, to the law and to the King. I swear to maintain with all my power the French Constitution, and especially the decrees relative to the Civil Constitution of the Clergy.'

The time fixed for the taking of this oath by all members of the clergy was immediately after High Mass on Sunday, January 16th, 1791, in the presence of the congregation and a representative of the General Council of the Commune. Failure to perform this obligation was to be punished by deprivation of stipend and loss of rights as an active citizen of the country. On December 26th, the imposition of the oath was sanctioned by the King. Louis may have hoped by his action to avert a schism between Church and State. In the event, he precipitated one.

From one-half to three-fifths of the clergy in the different departments took the oath.[1] Thirty bishops, led by La Rochefoucauld, had published on October 30th an 'Exposition of the Principles of the Civil Constitution of the Clergy' and demanded the immediate convocation of a National Council with subsidiary Provincial Councils to reexamine the whole question. The Pope was asked to intervene, but probably because of the implied gallicanism of the proposal, no satisfactory reply was received.

By February 5th, complete lists of the loyal clergy had been drawn up, and action was immediately taken against the dissenters. New clergy were elected in their places. On February 24th, Talleyrand consecrated the two new 'constitutional' bishops of Finistère and l'Aisne. On March 23rd nine more bishops were consecrated at Notre-Dame and on the following day Gobel was installed as Bishop of Paris. In the meantime, the dissenting priests were having an uncomfortable time. In the Departments of Finistère, Ile-et-Vilaine and Ain, they were forcibly compelled to withdraw at least four leagues from their old parishes. Nuns were beaten in the streets of Paris. In many parts of the country the dissenting clergy could practise their religion only in private.

On March 10th, the Pope publicly condemned the Civil Constitution of the Clergy. But, over-cautious, his intervention was too late to affect the course of events. The nationalisation of the Church had become a *fait accompli*. The Assembly felt so sure of itself that on May 7th, 1791, it decreed full liberty of conscience following upon Talleyrand's motion, that 'Liberty of conscience is a real and complete liberty, a real property, not less inviolable than any other and claiming full protection'. But public opinion still remained hostile to the nonjurors, and an attempt made by a number of them to attend Mass openly on Ascension Day, June 2nd, 1791, in the Church of the Théatins, was prevented by the mob, and only the speedy arrival of the National Guard and the personal intervention of Lafayette saved them from serious injury or worse.

One development, which was partially due to the conflict over Church affairs, and partially to the revolutionary fervour for the doctrines of the current *mystique*, was the growth of a new 'religion of reason'. Based on the philosophical teachings which had been fostered by the *sociétés de pensée* and the masonic lodges, and more

---

[1] Sagnac, from an examination of the lists of 43 departments, found that 14,047 clergy took the oath, whilst 10,395 did not. Cf. Aulard: *Christianity and the Revolution*, pp. 73, 74.

latterly by the ritual which had become common in the Jacobin clubs,[1] this religion of the fatherland took as its creed the Declaration of the Rights of Man, which was given the position commonly accorded to the Scriptures.   At services held in many parts of the country, it became not uncommon for an open-air service before the 'altar of the fatherland' to follow the celebration of Mass in the parish church.   At times, as at the Champ de Mars on July 14th, 1790, both services would take place before the same altar.

The new religion appears to have taken its strongest hold at Strasbourg, but it spread to almost every part of the country, not excepting Brittany.   In some cases, as in Alsace, children were given as many as three baptisms.   A Catholic child was given a Catholic godfather and a Protestant godmother, and baptised by the priest.   It was then given a Protestant godfather and a Catholic godmother, and baptised by the pastor.   This procedure was reversed in the case of a Protestant child. Finally, each child was given a civic baptism before the altar of the fatherland.   In this and other ways was given religious form to the teachings of the current *mystique* and its leading principle, the sovereignty of the nation.

The ecclesiastical policy of the Constitutional Group and the Left Wing had been designed to nationalise the Church in order to secure the removal of a possible source of disaffection.   The principle of the sovereignty of the 'general will' of the people had been invoked to justify the liquidation of a corporation whose separate, partial will could not be tolerated in the national State.   Its dissolution involved primarily the confiscation of its wealth, which conveniently relieved an economic and financial situation that was threatening to become desperate, and secondly the re-establishment of the Church as a Department of State.

But this, in turn, involved the popular election of bishops and clergy, as they had now become State servants, and thus further strengthened the Revolution by securing the compulsory submission of all candidates for posts in the Church to an electoral test conducted by the active citizens.   And as a final check upon the loyalty of the Church officials, an oath of allegiance to the new Constitution was imposed.   In this way, the Third Estate believed that it had largely protected itself against the danger of reactionary tendencies developing within the ranks of the clergy, and against the possibility of papal interference carried out through those members of the clergy who might still recognise the Pope as the sovereign power in ecclesiastical affairs.

[1] Cf. Brinton, op. cit., chapter on 'Religion'.

CHAPTER IX

THE CONTROL OF FOREIGN POLICY

IN no sphere of the political activities of the National Assembly does the distrust with which Louis XVI and his ministers were generally regarded become more apparent than in the field of foreign affairs. In particular, as the months went by, there developed a suspicion, amounting at a later date to a certainty, that Louis, Marie-Antoinette and the Court were secretly in negotiation with foreign powers in the hope of restoring the *status quo ante*. Equally, the growing menace of the reactionary *émigrés*, many of whom again were believed to be in secret communication with the Court, filled the deputies, and in particular those of the Left Wing, with disquiet and misgiving. In such a mood, little trust was placed by the majority of the Assembly either in the King or in the officials of the Foreign Office, from the Minister himself down to the ambassadors and even humbler members of the diplomatic service.

Again, on a wider plane, there existed a feeling that neither King nor Ministry could be entrusted, in their relations with foreign powers, with the correct interpretation of the spirit of the Revolution. At no time were the principles of the current *mystique* looked upon as having a purely national significance. In the debate preceding the formulation of the Declaration of Rights, deputy after deputy had born witness to their universal application, their relevance to all people in all lands. The embodiment of such principles in the conduct of foreign affairs would, it was generally believed, necessitate a revolution in diplomatic procedure. Sovereign people must speak to sovereign people. Only in this way would wars and rumours of wars be abolished forever. Only in this way would the tortuous channels of diplomatic intercourse, the rivalry of Kings for power and prestige, the ambitions of statesmen—characteristics of *l'ancien régime* which had led inevitably to recurrence of international conflict—be finally swept away. It could, therefore, be only a matter of time before the Assembly would find it necessary to intervene in what, until 1789, had been regarded as a prerogative of the King and his Ministry, the conduct of foreign relations.

On February 14th, 1787, Armand-Marc, Comte de Montmorin de Saint-Hérem, had been appointed by Louis to be Minister for Foreign Affairs. Montmorin had achieved his first major post in the diplomatic service in 1777, when he had become ambassador at Madrid. Later, in 1784, he had been made Commander-in-Chief in Brittany. Unlike most of the other ministers at the outbreak of the Revolution, he had achieved a certain amount of popularity with the Third Estate, due to his dismissal with Necker in July, 1789, and his subsequent return to office with that minister a few days later. In this way, he had identified himself in the minds of the deputies with the Revolution, a fact which was to stand him in good stead during the months which followed. But despite this initial popularity, it was to be Montmorin's misfortune that when things went badly in the sphere of foreign affairs, the deputies were equally to remember that he had held ministerial office in the days of *l'ancien régime* and that he had been a member of that *Conseil du Roi* which had, in 1787, opposed such reforms in the Estates General as common discussion between the Orders and the *vote par tête*. At such times he was destined to share in the obloquy which was directed against the ministers from 1790 onwards.

Montmorin never underestimated the importance of the National Assembly nor the strength of the principles with which it was imbued. As early as July 22nd, 1789, when rumours of war with England were in the air, he had sent a letter of reassurance to the Assembly, accompanied by one which he had received from the Duke of Dorset, protesting against the unwarrantable suspicions which had been directed against his government. The Assembly published both letters and expressed great satisfaction with the handling of the affair. Again, on August 4th, Montmorin sent a further letter of reassurance to the Assembly. By these actions, not only did Montmorin demonstrate his view that the Assembly had the right to be informed of all developments in foreign relations. He at the same time implied that the Assembly was the body from whom he was hereafter prepared to accept guidance and instruction. In this way, in the eyes of the deputies, he again acknowledged his recognition of the transfer of the sovereign power from the *salons* of Versailles to the *Salle des Menus Plaisirs*.[1]

---

[1] His private views were expressed to his friend de Ségur, who returned from St. Petersburg towards the end of 1789: 'On the one hand the people, in its ardour, seems to insist upon a democracy, which will lead to anarchy. It is up in arms against any who now wish to restrain it by legal means. On the other hand, the Court and the aristocracy by which the King is surrounded, reject obstinately

Apart from this trouble with England, there was little in the sphere of foreign relations during the remaining months of 1789 to divert the deputies from the more urgent affairs at home with which they were concerned.   In the event, the internal upheaval in France was generally regarded throughout Europe with satisfaction, as weakening that country in the military field.[1]   The German princes, for example, hailed with delight the 'eclipse of the sun at Versailles'.   Furthermore, the Great Powers themselves were either largely absorbed with other affairs, as was Prussia with Poland and Russia with the East, or they were recovering from a period of hostilities, as was England from the American war, and Austria from the effects of the Belgian Revolution and the war with Turkey.   Hence it was not until 1790 that the Assembly was constrained to consider the implications of the principles by which it was guided upon the conduct of foreign affairs.

The year 1790, however, was not destined to pass so peaceably for the Ministry of Foreign Affairs.   By February, there were signs of trouble with those German princes whose incomes, derived from their *fiefs* in Alsace and elsewhere, had been affected by the *arrêtés* of the night of August 4th, 1789, and by the decree of November 2nd of the same year which placed the wealth of the Church at the disposal of the nation.   A note from the *Cercle du Haut Rhin* was communicated to the Assembly by Montmorin on February 11th, an extract from which read, 'The deputies petition His Imperial Majesty and all influential circles in the Empire to accord protection to the Estates, to the nobility and clergy who are menaced.'

It is probable that the Assembly would have replied to the note in a somewhat cavalier fashion had not a similar situation developed in the Papal possessions of Avignon and the Comtat Venaissin, and as we have already noted, the deputies were anxious to avoid precipitating a crisis in this particular field whilst the Civil Constitution of the Clergy was

anything which does not contribute to the restoration of the "status quo ante". You know how I respect the King.   He is just, virtuous and good, but his goodness is deprived of all strength.   He is able to resist neither those he fears nor those he loves.   I continually make efforts, always in vain, to persuade him to follow some plan with firmness.'—de Ségur: *Mémoires*, Vol. III, p. 583, quoted Masson, F.: *Le Département des Affaires Étrangères pendant la Révolution, 1787–1804*, p. 71.

[1] Cf. Burke's speech in the House of Commons, February 9th, 1790: 'They (the French) have done their business for us as rivals in a way which twenty Ramillies and Blenheims could never have done.   Were we absolute conquerors, and France to be prostrate at our feet, we should be ashamed to send a commission to settle their affairs which would impose so hard a law upon the French, and one so destructive of all their consequence as a nation, as that which they have imposed upon themselves.'

under discussion.   Hence, despite the protests of Mirabeau,[1] the whole question was referred, on the motion of Goupil de Préfeln, to the Feudal Committee.

But this incident, together with the necessity for formulating a policy towards the growing revolt in the Papal possessions, compelled the Assembly to devote attention to the conduct of international affairs. The Left Wing in particular was emphatic about the necessity for bringing this branch of government activity more fully under the control and direction of the Assembly.   On May 14th, an opportunity occurred which enabled the Constitutional Group to take preliminary steps towards this end.   On this day, Montmorin had written to the Assembly informing them of increasing tension in view of the progress which England was making in an armaments drive directed against the possibility of war with Spain, and intimating that the King had ordered the re-equipment of fourteen warships to safeguard the realm.

Since the spring of 1789, England had been at cross-purposes with Spain over Nootka Sound, which she claimed the right to occupy despite Spain's assertions that it formed part of her own empire.   The Spaniards had captured a British vessel, and by the spring of 1790, it looked as though war was inevitable.   On May 5th, the British Government had mobilised the fleet, and, as a matter of course, the Spaniards appealed for French help in accordance with the terms of the Family Compact existing between the French Crown and the Bourbons of Spain and Italy.

The receipt of Montmorin's letter immediately precipitated a crisis in the Assembly.   On May 15th, the Duc de Biron had proposed a decree that 'The President should seek an audience with the King to thank him for the measures he has taken to secure the safety of the Empire and its commerce, and for the negotiations which he has undertaken.   He should also petition His Majesty to inform him of the needs of the naval authorities'.

Such a proposal provided the Left Wing with an excellent excuse for interfering in the affairs of the Ministry.   It was opposed as placing in doubt the sovereign power of the nation.   As Alexandre de Lameth said, 'We must consider whether the Assembly has the competence, and the sovereign nation the right, to delegate to the King the power of making war or concluding a peace.'   Other deputies affected to see in the King's action evidence of ministerial intrigue.   'The Ministers

[1] 'Your principles', he asserted, 'are not in accord with German public law but with nature.'

have sought to introduce discord into the Assembly,' declared Duquesnoy; 'they are trying to destroy its unity . . . Before everything else, we must ask ourselves: Can the King do this? Must he do that? Can we do this? Must we do that?' In an effort to gain breathing space, the Right Wing tried to secure a postponement of the debate for three weeks. But the proposal was shouted down, Barnave declaring that it was yet another plot.

Several Right Wing deputies attempted a defence of the Ministry, but one of their speakers, Goupil de Préfeln, was rudely interrupted by de Broglie. 'It is vital that you demonstrate to all nations that we, the French nation, basing our conduct on principles very different from those which, in the past, have resulted in so much misery for so many peoples, wish to avoid all wars and to live in that brotherly concord with them which is in accord with the precepts of nature. It is to the interest of all nations to protect the French nation, because it is from France that human liberty and the happiness of the whole world must flow.' He questioned the right of the King to take any steps, even of a purely defensive character, which might become a latent cause of war. This was a matter purely for the representatives of the sovereign nation.

Mirabeau took up the same theme. Whilst urging the necessity for immediate action in view of the danger to the security of the country, he insisted that the whole question of the King's right to decide on peace or war should be fully examined. He also launched a tirade against the Ministry, which in his view had seriously abused its powers. It is probable that at this stage Mirabeau was manœuvring to secure a lever with which to strengthen his dealings with the Court, which at this moment had reached a critical stage.

The members of the extreme Left Wing were opposed to the King's influence upon the conduct of foreign relations for rather different reasons. They feared that were the King to be victorious in a war, he would become a potential threat to the Revolution. On this ground, many deputies went further than the Left Centre were prepared to go, in insisting that full control of such a power must be vested in its natural depositary, the representative assembly of the sovereign people. Reubell and d'Aiguillon both made speeches along these lines, the last named emphasising that 'A victorious King constitutes a grave danger to liberty, above all when he is a King of France.'

The Left Centre Group was equally determined to secure that the ultimate control of foreign policy should rest with the legislative body, but they were not prepared to remove from the King those of his functions which were his attribute as head of the executive power in the State. Their object, as we have already seen, was to preserve the Monarchy but to constitutionalise the King. The principle of the separation of powers, to which the Group had paid lip service, necessitated the retention by the King of certain functions. Thus whilst the Constitutionalists were prepared to remove from royal control so vital an issue as the right of peace and war, they were not prepared to take away entirely from the King the conduct of foreign relations, providing such conduct were adequately supervised by the legislature.

After some further discussion the Assembly ultimately decided to approve the measures which had been taken by the King, but also to examine fully the whole question of the power of the King in relation to the right of declaring war or making peace. The motion was Mirabeau's: 'The President shall immediately seek an audience with the King to thank His Majesty for the measures he has taken to maintain peace. Tomorrow, however, we shall debate the following important constitutional question—should the nation delegate the right of declaring war or concluding a peace to the King.'

Thus was the stage cleared for the combat. Already the Paris mob was showing signs of impatience. At the Jacobin Club, Montmorin's letter to the Assembly had already been condemned as a manœuvre to divide and disturb the deputies. Carra, writing in the *Annales Patriotiques*, put the Jacobin point of view: 'The right to make peace and to declare war, as also to make foreign alliances,' he wrote, 'belongs to the nation, and it is for the National Assembly alone to decide what action should be taken in view of recent occurrences.' He then went on to point out that in his opinion, the whole affair was a plot on the part of the Ministry to bring about a war with the avowed purpose of embarrassing the work of the Assembly, discrediting the assignats, ruining the trade of the ports and the commerce of the country and ultimately, by bringing about national bankruptcy, destroying the new Constitution. 'Citizens,' he concluded, 'we have formed ourselves into patriotic societies. Let us, then, close our ranks and raise a powerful voice against the perfidy of the ministers; let us drive them from the presence of a King who is everlastingly infected by their aristocratic venom. Why should we delay in getting rid of these insolent and incapable persons? . . . We wish to be the friend of all nations, the enemy of all tyrants.   We will recognise no family compacts but those made by national families.'

In the Assembly, the debate was opened by the Duc de Lévis, who proposed four questions as the basis for discussion.

Primarily, would the French nation, as a matter of principle, ever endanger the liberty of any other nation?   Secondly, was the executive power alone to be charged with the defence of the Kingdom?   What degree of responsibility should be left to the Ministry?   In the third place, who should be charged with the task of concluding a peace? And finally, should alliances which had already been contracted with foreign powers be ratified by the Assembly?

It was soon apparent that the Right Wing was divided on these issues.   The deputies of the extreme Right Wing opposed any interference with the right of the King to conduct international affairs. Cazalès, in a lengthy speech, insisted that the conduct of foreign affairs necessitated secrecy, speed and cunning, and that it was impossible for a numerous assembly to control such delicate operations.   He was supported by the Comte de Sérent, who said, 'Large assemblies are little suited to handle political matters. . . .   How can foreign affairs be conducted in an assembly which is primarily political in character?' The elder Mirabeau made a rather different point.   'The right to declare war and dispose our forces must always be vested in the supreme executive of the general will of the nation.'   Other Right Wing deputies, including Sinnetti, de Bousmard, Virieu, La Galissonnière, Montlosier, the Abbé de Montesquiou, Clermont-Tonnerre, the Duc de Praslin, the Abbé Maury and the Duc du Châtelet, all stressed the view that to remove the right of making war or peace from the King was to reduce the executive power to a mere shadow.   The same arguments had been advanced in the earlier debates on the relationships between the legislative and executive powers.   But most of these deputies were prepared to grant the Assembly the right to negotiate commercial treaties, and several of them were prepared to uphold the right of the legislature to be consulted before any cession of national territory was made by the King.

On the other hand, the Right Centre Group, composed mainly of what was left of the Monarchists, took a more moderate view.   Thus Malouet compromised by suggesting that whilst the Assembly alone should have the power to order the declaration of an offensive war, the executive should be given the right to set up legitimate military defences, and to take immediate and appropriate action when the property of the nation should be threatened. Again, he considered that the King should have the power to conclude treaties with other nations, subject to a reservation that the Assembly should review any treaty before signature if it contained any provision for an increase or cession of national territory.

The point of view of the Constitutionalists was best put by Mirabeau. He argued that whilst the right of peace and war undoubtedly belonged to the nation, it had necessarily to be delegated concurrently to the legislative body and to the executive power. To the King should belong the conduct of diplomatic relations and the control and disposal of the army and the navy. In the event of war appearing possible, it was the duty of the King, through his ministers, to notify the legislature. The legislature should retain control of the National Guard and, as a matter of right, approve all treaties entered into by the King before they were put into execution.

Mirabeau's argument was feebler than that of Malouet, and it came in for strong criticism from the Right Wing. The Archbishop of Aix, d'Estourmil, Goupil de Préfeln and Cazalès all opposed it on the ground that it left to the King no more than a fictitious power.

It was also opposed by a small number of deputies of the Left Centre, led by Le Chapelier, who seceded from the ranks of the Constitutionalists on this issue on the ground that the principle of the separation of powers necessitated the retention by the King of real power concerning war and peace, and who were therefore inclined to support Malouet's proposals. But the vast majority of the members of the Left were too distrustful of the King, too suspicious of the suspected machinations of the Ministry, and too afraid of the possibility of foreign intervention and of the manœuvres of the *émigrés*, to allow the control of foreign affairs and the disposition of the armed forces of the country to be entirely divorced from their authority. To justify this view, the doctrine of the sovereignty of the 'general will' was once more invoked. The people had replaced the King as the sovereign power. They therefore fell heir to all power which had previously vested in the Crown. And the 'general will' of the people could be discovered only in the assembly of its representatives.

It was the same tenet of the current *mystique* which had been the *leit motif* of the Left Wing throughout their constitution-making activities. 'The right of declaring the general will', insisted Charles de Lameth, 'belongs only to the representatives of the nation. Therefore the right of peace and war belongs to the nation alone, by the principles of the Constitution. . . .' He went on to accuse the Right Wing of desiring to foment a war to arrest the Revolution. 'If they have the gold,' he concluded, 'we have the steel, and we shall know how to use it.' The *curé* Jallet went further. 'The right of peace and war', he declared, 'does not belong to any one nation, but to all nations. If all nations were free, there would be no war. The right of any one nation to examine the motives likely to lead to war is an essential attribute of its sovereign power. It resides essentially in the nation. The nation must retain the exercise of this right and cannot delegate it to the King.'

Barnave strongly supported Jallet's argument. 'I do not speak of the sovereignty of the people,' he said, 'for this has been consecrated in the Declaration of Rights. When, however, you commenced to draw up the Constitution, you began to apply this majestic principle. And from this flows logically the right of the representatives of the people to declare war, which is essentially an act to be determined by the general will of the people.' Many other deputies reiterated similar arguments, d'Aiguillon even proposing that the time was ripe to formulate an international Declaration of Rights.

Many of the speeches of the extreme Left were directed against the ministers. Reubell declaimed against 'these wars fomented by ministers, waged without the consent of the people, which shed their blood and waste their money'. Pétion condemned the Ministry for having entered into a Family Compact at all. D'Aiguillon was of the opinion that if the conduct of foreign affairs were left to the King and his ministers, 'ministerial intrigues would continue unchecked, the citizens would continue to be deceived, and the ministers would continue to profit equally from our disasters as from our successes'. De Custine demanded that any minister found guilty of having provoked an unnecessary war should be condemned to death.

Despite his earlier popularity with the Assembly, Montmorin did not escape the criticism which was thus levelled at the ministers generally. Barnave and the de Lameths—the so-called Triumvirate —made especially vicious attacks upon him. 'Can the nation be other than disquieted, when this man, whose actions concern us all, remains so closely associated with the Court? asked Alexandre de Lameth. 'Was not this minister summoned to the King's Council at a time when the National Assembly was surrounded with bayonets?' Montmorin was, however, strongly defended by Goupil de Préfeln and by the Duc du Châtelet, amongst other Right Wing deputies.

The extreme Left Wing was particularly concerned with the fundamental principles upon which, these deputies insisted, the whole problem of the conduct of foreign relations rested. Robespierre could not believe that wars were ever made by peoples. Were the principle of popular sovereignty to be applied in other nations, he could not conceive that war would ever break out, a point of view which was subsequently held up to scorn by Malouet, who insisted that in the past more wars had been made by free peoples than by despots. But Robespierre's argument was taken up by de Lévis, who concluded an eloquent address by proposing that the Assembly should declare, in a most solemn manner, that it would never threaten the rights of other peoples, but that it would repulse, with all the courage of a free people, any attempt which might be made against its own rights.

Pétion de Villeneuve attacked all forms of secret diplomacy, all *ressorts cachés* and *fils imperceptibles*. Mystery resulted in injustices; it produced grave political errors. 'It is to the clandestine intrigues of the ministers', he declared, 'that all our misfortunes are to be attributed.'

So the debate proceeded. There was never any doubt as to its outcome; the great majority of the deputies supported the Left Centre in its mistrust of ministerial intrigue, in its suspicion of the secret activities of the Court, in its fear that foreign intervention might be secured in order to sabotage the Revolution. But equally they were afraid of the growing radicalism of the extreme Left Wing, of the increasing restiveness and lawlessness of the Paris mob. At all costs it was necessary to preserve the monarchical machine, the constitutional form of the government, by preserving to the King a titular authority. As a result of this, the Assembly decided on May 22nd, 1790, that whilst the duty of ensuring the safety of the Kingdom, of making preparations for war proportioned by the known or suspected preparations of other States, of conducting foreign diplomatic relations and of choosing and appointing the ministers should be delegated to the King, the right of peace and war belonged to the legislative body alone. Where by reason of urgency, hostilities should have been commenced in order to support an ally or to preserve national rights, it was the King's duty to summon the legislature immediately, whereupon the legislature would decide whether the war should be carried on or stopped. Should the legislative body subsequently judge that the war had been brought about as a measure of aggression by a minister or his agents, the 'guilty author of such hostility' should be adjudged guilty of the crime of *lèse-majesté* and suitably punished.

Thus, whilst granting titular authority to the executive, and so paying lip service to the doctrine of the separation of the powers of government, the Assembly had once again secured for itself all real control of the conduct of foreign relations. As Cazalès remarked bitterly, 'It is necessary to let the people into a secret. There is no longer any King.'

But these decrees did not go far enough to satisfy the extreme Left Wing or the Paris mob. When they became known, Right Wing deputies were maltreated on their way to the Assembly; Mirabeau was attacked in the street, whilst on all sides the cry of *le grand trahison du comte de Mirabeau* was raised.[1] The position was summed up by Fréron in his *Orateur du Peuple*. 'If the right of declaring war and concluding peace had been placed in the hands of the King,' he wrote, 'civil war would have broken out on Saturday night, and today Paris would be bathed in blood. At midnight, the tocsin would have called the citizens to arms; the château of the Tuileries would have been put to the flames; the people would have taken the monarch and his family into protective custody, but Saint-Priest, Necker, Montmorin and La Luzerne would have been hanged and their heads carried in procession through the city.'

On May 24th, Mirabeau proposed that a further item should be added to the decrees of May 22nd, requiring that all treaties and conventions then in existence should be examined by a special committee which would decide whether or not they should be ratified by the Assembly. Mirabeau's action was probably designed to create yet another lever by which he could further his machinations with the Court. Nevertheless, it had the support of Robespierre, who believed that all foreign commitments entered into by the country were a fruitful source of war, and opposed to the essentially peaceful policy of the new régime. After some discussion, however, the proposition was rejected by the Assembly, following a speech by Fréteau in which he pointed out that the time was highly inopportune for any such revision of foreign alliances.

But this matter was again to be brought to the notice of the Assembly before two more months had elapsed. The growing reconciliation of the European powers had made increased progress since the Emperor Leopold had succeeded his brother Joseph II in February, 1790. At Reichenbach, on June 26th, 1790, a meeting, arranged by Frederick William of Prussia, between the representatives of the

[1] Cf. Masson, op. cit., p. 79.

Emperor and those of England and Holland, had led to the mutual adoption by these countries of a more friendly attitude the one to the other. At the same time, Austria had quietened Belgian restiveness by granting her certain liberal guarantees, whilst on August 14th, Catherine II of Russia had signed the Peace of Verela with Gustavus III of Sweden. Thus the various factors which had previously prevented the Great Powers from uniting against France had been largely resolved and the Continent was now free to turn its attention to the menace presented by the new revolutionary régime in France.

Mirabeau had warned the Assembly against this danger. 'Perpetual peace remains a dream, and a dangerous dream,' he declared, 'if it led to the disarmament of France whilst Europe remained in arms.' But the Assembly had disregarded this advice, although certain other deputies appreciated the danger, and one of them wrote, on July 5th, 1790: 'We will soon have a Constitution, and we may have corn, but in my view war will soon carry off our corn, our Constitution and our *assignats*.'

And the seeds of war were by no means lacking in the summer of 1790. Primarily, the possessors of *fiefs* in Alsace, including the Princes of Württemberg, Deux-Ponts and Baden, had all vehemently protested against the *arrêtés* of August 4th, 1789, which had abolished their feudal rights in this province. On April 28th, 1790, the Feudal Committee of the Assembly, to whom their protest had been referred, had accepted the principle of an indemnity,[1] but when this had failed to satisfy the princes, who refused to sacrifice their seigniorial rights, the Committee had reported as follows: 'The National Assembly, in the belief that throughout the French Empire there cannot be any other sovereign power than the general will of the nation, hereby declares that all its decrees relative to Seigniorial and Feudal Rights will be enforced in the departments of the Upper and Lower Rhine, as in all other parts of the kingdom.'

This further inflamed the princes, who thereupon decided to carry the whole affair to the Diet of Ratisbon. Secondly, there was the latent hostility between France and the Papacy which had been fanned by the revolt in Avignon and the Comtat Venaissin, which had broken out on June 12th. The papal legate had been expelled and

---

[1] *Moniteur Universel*, 1790, p. 485. The recommendation ran as follows: 'Que le Roi sera prié de faire négocier avec les dits Princes une détermination aimable des indemnités qui leur seront accordées pour raison des Droits Seignioriaux et Féodaux abolis par les dits Décrets.'

the people had voted their incorporation with France. The Assembly had hesitated to give a verdict as they were still anxious to use this possible loss to the Papacy of rights and revenues as a lever to secure the Pope's blessing on the Civil Constitution of the Clergy. And finally, the King of Prussia had started an active campaign in Central Europe against the 'hereditary enemy' which on more than one occasion had burned the Palatinate.

The Assembly did not realise the extent to which the situation had deteriorated until July 27th, when Dubois-Crancé read letters purporting to show that the frontier posts were inadequately manned, and that the inhabitants of the frontier towns, disaffected by their close proximity to the sources of counter-revolution, were ready to permit the passage of foreign troops. Then Fréteau, despite the fact that he had previously opposed Mirabeau on this very question, insisted that the treaty position should be reviewed, adding that it was his belief that for the past thirty years they had all operated to the disadvantage of the country. He demanded that the Assembly send for Montmorin and interrogate him on existing commitments. He was supported by Voidel, who considered that the whole of Europe was in league against France.

Ultimately Muguet proposed that six commissioners should call upon Montmorin, and examine with him the treaty position. He was supported by Reubell and by d'André, who suggested that the committee should be given the name of 'Committee of Foreign Affairs'. The Assembly carried the proposition with enthusiasm and immediately elected Fréteau, Dubois-Crancé, Menou, d'Elbecq, d'André and Emeric to the Committee. They were required to 'repair without delay to the Ministry of Foreign Affairs and to demand to see all communications which had been sent or received, which related in any way to the diplomatic situation existing between France and her neighbouring countries'.

In this way, the Constitutionalists took another step towards the goal whose attainment they now regarded as essential—the control of foreign affairs. Through such a committee they could exercise continuous surveillance not only over the conduct of international relations, but over the Ministry, and through the Ministry, over the King. Having established, in the name of the sovereign people, control over the internal affairs of the State, not excepting the affairs of the Church, they were now in a position to secure control over the external affairs of the country. They had thus placed the ascendancy of the Third

Estate, so they believed, beyond the danger of armed opposition secretly fostered by a hostile executive and a strongly reactionary Court.

As a result of researches conducted principally by Fréteau, with the willing co-operation of Montmorin, the Committee, on July 29th, reached the conclusion that the time was over-ripe for the establishment of a further committee to examine all foreign treaties and report thereon to the Assembly within eight days. Such a committee was to be further charged with the task of formulating steps to secure the safety of the Kingdom.

A last effort was made by the Right Wing to prevent the committee from being formed. Amongst many deputies, Regnaud and de Noailles denounced it in violent terms as utterly unconstitutional. But the extreme Left Wing wanted to go even further. Buzot, for example, was anxious that the Committee should be empowered to examine all the acts of the Ministry since the Assembly had been constituted. Ultimately it was decided, on Emeric's proposition, that the new committee should consist of six deputies, and that it should be 'required to take cognisance of all treaties in existence between France and foreign countries, and of any engagements which had resulted from them, and to render an account of them to the Assembly'. The members of the Committee elected were Fréteau, Menou, Mirabeau, Châtelet, d'André and Barnave. The Committee became known as the Diplomatic Committee.

Almost immediately trouble broke out over the Spanish affair. On August 2nd, Montmorin announced that English rearmament against Spain was continuing, that Spain had again asked for implementation of the Family Compact, and that he would be glad if the Assembly would appoint a committee to confer with him on the matter. The Diplomatic Committee lay to hand, and it immediately started work to such good purpose that by November 25th, when Spain and England came to terms, it had fully established itself as a governmental committee with power to keep under constant surveillance the work of the Ministry.

Montmorin had preserved much of his early popularity by his readiness to meet the Assembly and facilitate the work of the Diplomatic Committee. He therefore succeeded in escaping much of the obloquy which was showered on his brother ministers towards the end of 1790.[1] By this time, under the pressure of the more radical deputies and of the mob, whose passions were inflamed by the popular

---

[1] A violent attack was made upon him on November 10th by Danton, as leader of a deputation from the Paris Commune, but this was refuted in the Assembly.

press and the orators of the Palais Royal, doubts as to the loyalty of the King's ministers had come to a head. Even the Foreign Office did not escape criticism. On November 17th, the Left Wing decided to extend the procedure which it had decided to employ in the case of the dissenting clergy—to insist that all ambassadors, King's messengers, resident officials, consuls and vice-consuls, their secretaries and other employees, as well as the ministers themselves, should be required to take an oath of allegiance to the new régime. In this way, as in the case of the clergy, it was hoped to eliminate all persons whose loyalty to the Revolution might be in doubt. The oath read as follows—'I swear to be faithful to the nation, to the law and to the King, to maintain with all my power the Constitution decreed by the National Assembly, and to protect (in the country of ——) Frenchmen who shall there be found.'

The document containing the oath was to be signed and sealed with the seal of the chancellery or embassy or agency to which the official was attached. Instant dismissal was to follow the refusal of any official to take the oath. On December 30th, 1790, Montmorin supplied the Assembly with a list of the officials who had taken the oath. Very few had refused, but notable exceptions were de Bernis at Rome, de Bombelles at Venice and de Castellane at Geneva. They were all instantly recalled.

The year 1791 opened with a further attack by the Left Wing on the personnel of the Foreign Office. On January 28th, again at the instigation of Mirabeau, they decided upon a purge of their diplomatic representatives abroad. Mirabeau argued that it was essential to employ in this delicate work only 'men who would not compromise the authority of the nation by creating doubts as to its strength and purpose, who would not be hostile to the new international outlook which it was their duty to interpret, and who would not through ignorance, or by reason of their prejudices due to long experience of serving a despotism, be unable to rise to the heights of interpreting a system of government based on freedom'. At this time there can be no doubt that Mirabeau was working closely with Montmorin,[1] who hastened to apply the Assembly's decree to such good purpose that by March 27th he had secured royal approval for seven new major appointments in the diplomatic service.[2] By way of return, Mirabeau

[1] Cf. Masson, op. cit., p. 88.
[2] De Ségur (Rome), de Vibraye (Stockholm), de Durfort (Venice), d'Osmond (St. Petersburgh), de Gouvernat (The Hague), de Montesquiou (Dresden) and de Bonne-Carrière (Liège).

supported Montmorin in the Assembly on at least two important occasions. As the foreign situation appeared to become more and more threatening, the extreme Left Wing seized every chance to attack Montmorin, and when, on March 13th, he announced the opening of military negotiations with Switzerland, and again on March 17th, when he demanded the strengthening of the northern frontier defences, it was Mirabeau's influence alone which saved him from severe criticism.

The reason for Mirabeau's support for Montmorin is explained in his notes to the Court, in which Montmorin was cited as the only minister the deputies would listen to, and that he alone could be the centre of that secret ministry of which Mirabeau was to be the head.[1]

But the more radical deputies could never forget that Montmorin had served the King in the days of *l'ancien régime*, and when Mirabeau's death lost him his principal advocate in the Assembly, he suffered in the violent attack which was made upon the Ministry generally after April 6th. Menou made a particularly virulent attack upon him for his choice of officials, none of whom, he insisted, showed enthusiasm for the Revolution. Buzot, in turn, insisted upon the right of the legislature, as the sovereign body in the State, to dismiss all ministers who had conducted themselves as badly as had Montmorin. Despite Robespierre's support for Buzot's proposal, the Left Centre, for reasons which we have discussed in an earlier chapter, were not prepared to concede such a right.

But under continuous pressure from the mob, who had become more and more agitated as the debate on ministerial responsibility proceeded, the deputies of the Left Centre had increasing difficulty in maintaining their position. Typical of much journalistic comment was that of an article in *L'Orateur du Peuple*, which asserted that if the King left the capital, Montmorin would resign, foreign powers would attack by land and sea and chaos would ensue. As a result, the King was forcibly prevented by the mob from taking his Easter Communion at St. Cloud, an event which brought him to the Assembly in protest and to assert his right to leave the capital.

On April 19th, the extreme Left Wing found another opportunity to attack Montmorin. A letter had been received by the Assembly from the Estates of Porentruy denouncing the movement of troops belonging to the Bishop of Bâle, and requesting that the French immediately occupy this territory. Whilst Reubell attacked Mont-

[1] Cf. Masson, op. cit., p. 89.

morin, Babet directed his attack against the Diplomatic Committee. D'André defended the Committee by asserting that it did not possess the power to participate directly in the functions of the Ministry of Foreign Affairs. Menou defended the Committee by asserting that Montmorin was an extremely difficult minister to work with.

But Reubell and Babet were supported by Robespierre, who protested against the activities of enemy agents, declared that the ministers were inactive, and complained that the Diplomatic Committee was not keeping a sufficiently close watch upon Montmorin, and was not revealing secret information in its possession which was of the greatest importance to the nation. Robespierre in turn was supported by Pétion de Villeneuve and Louis de Noailles.

In view of these continued attacks, Montmorin advised the King to address a letter to all ambassadors and foreign agents of the country re-affirming his adherence to the principles of the Revolution which, in the words of the letter despatched on April 23rd, consisted in 'the annihilation of a mass of abuses which had accumulated over the centuries through the errors of the people or the power of ministers who had not been controlled by the King'. He further asserted that he was free—absolutely free and absolutely happy. His letter terminated with praise of the new Constitution, 'which, by ensuring the liberty and equality of all citizens, had founded the national prosperity on unshakeable foundations; which bounded the royal authority by the law; which had prevented, by a glorious revolution, that other revolution which the abuses of *l'ancien régime* would have made inevitable and which would have led to the dissolution of the Empire'.

As Chabroud remarked, after the text of this letter had been read in the Assembly, 'For the first time, the sacred maxims which codify the rights of man have been included in diplomatic correspondence.' But outside the Assembly, Marat,[1] Stanislas Girardin[2] and the Abbé Royau[3] all ridiculed the sentiments which it contained, and doubts as to Montmorin's integrity remained. He was, for example, accused of having written this letter to throw sand into the eyes of the people.

On June 5th, however, Montmorin became hopelessly compromised. At the request of the Russian minister, he had issued two passports, one for the Baroness de Korff, a *valet de chambre*, two

---

[1] He drew attention to the fact that only five days earlier Louis XVI had visited the Assembly to plead 'comme un écolier' for his freedom to leave Paris.

[2] In an article in the *Ami du Peuple*, Girardin found the King 'too revolutionary' (No. 443).

[3] *Réflexions de l'abbé Royau*—an eight-page pamphlet.

children and three servants, and the other for a Baroness de Stegleman, her daughter, a valet and three servants, all travelling to Frankfurt. They were the passports for the Royal Family, whose flight to Varennes was discovered on June 21st.

Montmorin was besieged in his house by the mob, and he was compelled to ask the Assembly for guards to protect him and to enable him to visit the Assembly. These were granted, and after an eloquent speech in which he protested his innocence the Assembly was sufficiently mollified to ask him to prepare a report on the foreign situation. But when, a little later, the affair of the passports became known, Montmorin had to fight for his life. Attacked by Biauzat, Camus, Reubell and other Left Wing deputies, it was only with the utmost difficulty that he succeeded once again in asserting his innocence.

From this time onward the Diplomatic Committee took over the detailed supervision of the Foreign Office, and Fréteau, the spokesman of the Committee, answered all questions in the Assembly relating to foreign affairs. In the final draft of the Constitution, the decrees proposed by the Left Centre Group, which we examined earlier in this chapter, were inserted without change. Despite Varennes, the Constitutionalists were determined to reinstate the King as head of the Executive Power, whilst ensuring that, at every turn, the real power lay with the legislative body.

Thus, in the sphere of foreign relations, as in the entire field of internal affairs, the Left Centre Group had succeeded in securing the dependence of the executive upon the legislature. At any time, the Foreign Minister could be summoned before the bar of the Assembly, and sent for trial before a criminal court for what the legislature chose to regard as *un délit coupable*. In this way, the Constitutional Group believed that it had eliminated the possibility of external attempts to sabotage the system established by the Third Estate, as it had equally prevented internal dissension designed to achieve a similar purpose. In foreign affairs, as in home affairs, the sovereignty of the people, the omnipotence of the 'general will', as crystallised in the representative legislature, had been invoked to overcome all opposition to the new régime.

CHAPTER X

CONCLUSION

WHAT, then, did the Constituent Assembly succeed in achieving? The answer to this question is written large in the Constitution of 1791. It sought to establish the security, as also the supremacy, of bourgeois property right. And in the political field this meant government of the people by the Third Estate in the primary interest of the bourgeoisie and incidentally, so it was generally believed, in the interest of the people as a whole, who could not fail to benefit from such an enlightened rule. In this sense it is probably not sufficient to accuse the Third Estate of legislating purely in the interests of a group. Without doubt, the interests of the group were placed first. But it was accepted by the majority of deputies in the Assembly that these particular interests reflected the common interest of the nation as a whole.

The Assembly had successfully opposed the establishment of a democracy in the modern sense of the word. What in reality emerged from the legislation of 1789–91 was rather a plutocracy based on the retention of all real power by a wealthy commercial, industrial and *rentier* class, which nevertheless was clothed in the garments of democracy.

The disputes which occurred between the Constitutionalists, who were in a majority, and the more radical Left Wing, who formed a vociferous minority, were essentially disputes as to the limitations which were to be imposed upon the selected group. The Left Wing in general demanded an extension of the limits of this group to include the small property-owner, the 'little man', whereas the main body of deputies thought in terms of a more powerful, 'entrepreneurial' class whose main interest it was to free the profit motive from institutional restriction, to create an environment which no longer constituted a challenge to the *laisser-faire* ideology.

But institutional change could not be accomplished in the face of vested privilege unless the tenets of the doctrine of such change were given the aspect of universality. And how could appeal be made to that mass of the people, upon whose support the success of political change clearly depended, in terms of the glowing benefits which could be secured by free capitalistic expansion, unfettered trade and unrestricted private enterprise? It is possible that a good case could have been made out on such a basis, but it would have suffered from two vital weaknesses. Primarily, it would have savoured too much of class legislation, of an attempt to consummate the particular interests of a selected group. As such it would have been vulnerable not only to mass criticism, but to the attack of vested privilege itself, which may have secured in the process the co-opposition of the Fourth Estate. Secondly, the mass of the people, illiterate and uninformed, smarting under feudal burdens and economic inequalities, could scarcely have been trusted to perceive that their own interests were bound up with those of the capitalist group. Why should they have done so? To the artisan, the capitalist meant the tax-gatherer, the encloser of land, the violator of the *droit de vaine pâture*.

It was therefore necessary for the Third Estate to seek to secure their aims by intertwining them with those universal, imprescriptible truths, capable of withstanding any attack as fundamental attributes of man as man, in whose name the whole existing political structure could be undermined. Such truths lay to hand. They were the leading tenets of a philosophy of change, born of long-term dissatisfaction with the existing order, which had swept Western Europe, and in particular France, and which had spread across the ocean to the New World. They were familiar to the illiterate masses, they were embodied in the new religion, they permeated the political thought of men in all walks of life. They remained unaffected by the storied march of history for they had their roots deep in the prehistory of man. Natural Right preceded Divine Right. Natural Liberty and Natural Law pointed inevitably to the natural sovereignty of the people as a whole. Man prostituted himself to no man, but himself formed part of the sovereign community. Such were the doctrines. Such was the political religion.

The tenets of this philosophy had their roots in the growing resistance to the principle of an absolute monarchy which had slowly permeated political thought in France during the eighteenth century. For more than half a century confined to intellectual circles, attempts by the nobility and the *parlements* from 1750 onwards to increase their authority at the expense of enfeebled monarchs had led to a growth of political consciousness among the bourgeoisie, which was heightened by their virtual exclusion from any control over the government of the country. The pretensions of the *parlements* and the nobility were therefore soon outmatched by the political demands of the Third Estate, which demands were given the aspect of universalism by the support which they derived from the leading philosophers of the century. During the last quarter of the century, and in particular during the years immediately preceding the convocation of the Estates General, this new philosophy had been so popularised by subsidiary writers and by discussion in the *sociétés de pensée* and elsewhere that it had assumed the proportions of a *mystique*, based upon a new conception of the rights of man and the sovereignty of the 'general will' of the people. Thus, when the Estates General met in 1789, the Third Estate had behind it the support of the masses, imbued with a revolutionary fervour based on an incomplete and often adulterated concept of the new philosophy which was not, for that reason, less effective.

In its spiritual emphasis this philosophy had the strength of a new faith. It was to France what the Scriptures were to the Puritans, the Communist Manifesto to the Russian proletariat. It was basic, it was national. More, it was international, universal. Prior to 1789, it had lain dormant; its principles were abstract, indeterminate. The summoning of the Estates General to meet at Versailles was the match which lit the fuse. It remained for the Third Estate so to direct this fuse that what may have become a major conflagration was confined to the minor destruction alone of all that was incompatible with the policy of the new régime and all that this implied.

The Third Estate seized upon this new religion, harnessed it and ultimately succeeded in guiding it into channels wherein it could be powerfully employed in the interests of their own particular group. In this they were both successful and unsuccessful. They were successful in that they largely succeeded in securing mass support for the legislation which was embodied in the Constitution of 1791, which was in every respect a bourgeois charter. They were enabled to do this by ensuring the identification of every law they passed with the tenets of the new religion, by justifying their action in terms of the universal interest. This made any opposition savour of blasphemy; it made an enemy of the Assembly an enemy of the State.

They were unsuccessful in that the very power which they exploited was to prove too powerful for them. Other groups, including that more progressive and ultra-democratic group led by Robespierre, had learned the trick. The Girondins were to fall because of their moderation, because of their desire to set a limit to change. And later, under the pressure of external hostility and the increasing restiveness of the nation, the Jacobins were themselves to split into a moderate and a more progressive group. It was, as it were, as though the dam once loosed, the waters of progress had to expend their power. Each successive effort to curb this power failed until the force had largely expended itself. And then, amid the havoc of the flood, illumined brightly by the sun of liberty and warmed by a glowing consciousness of the newly recognised worth of the individual, came the dictator Napoleon, to build upon the ruins. But the political face of the country was indissolubly changed. The tenets of the new freedom remained to be spread by the Napoleonic armies. The principles established in 1791 were to remain a powerful political force throughout the nineteenth century.

The Constituent Assembly, then, first harnessed the flood, and possibly for this reason its work has longest stood the test of time. Of the fruits of its legislative activity, modified and partially destroyed within a matter of months, much has remained. The Declaration of the Rights of Man and of the Citizen still stands as a supreme charter in the minds of Frenchmen, revolutionary and anti-revolutionary, conservative and progressive alike. Once the step had been taken, it could never be retraced. The forces of change and progress, although for more than a century to be confined within the narrower channels of group interest, yet embodied all the essentials of a wider democracy, and of a universal freedom amongst men.

But the Constituent Assembly, anxious to set a limit to change, nevertheless miscalculated the strength of the forces which had been released. It did not realise the extent to which it had become identified in the public mind with a treacherous king; it had failed to recognise that by legislating primarily in the interests of *la haute bourgeoisie*, it had been branded by Paris as aiming at a plutocracy with royalist sympathies. Within three years these forces were to burst the banks within which they had temporarily been confined. The Commune and the Terror were the camp-followers of the Constituents.

In two years, however, the National Assembly had established the principles of democratic government for the first time on the continent of Europe. Others were to build on the foundation which was laid down in 1791. And today, the rallying-cry of Frenchmen everywhere is the historic Declaration of 1789, with its basic, *Les hommes naissent et demeurent libres et égaux en droits.* The Constitution of 1791 was a bourgeois triumph, but it was also a necessary step in the protracted march of mankind towards that ideal of political, economic and social freedom which must remain the inevitable goal of all human striving.

APPENDIX

FROCHOT'S SCHEME FOR REVISION OF THE CONSTITUTION, SUBMITTED TO THE ASSEMBLY ON AUGUST 31ST, 1791

OF NATIONAL SOVEREIGNTY, THE EXERCISE OF WHICH IS NOT PERMANENTLY DELEGATED

CHAPTER ONE

Of Partial Reformation and of the Amendment of the Constitution

Section One

Of the Power of the Nation in this Respect, and of its Delegation

The nation, in which all sovereignty resides, has the power to reform the Constitution in part, or that of changing it as a whole.

When it pleases it to exercise one or the other of these powers, it delegates it

In the first instance to a National Convention,

In the second instance to a Constituent Body.

Section Two

Of the National Convention

The National Convention is the Assembly of representatives having the right to revise, and the power to reform by changes, suppressions or additions, one or more determined parts of the Constitution.

It cannot be called upon to touch the fundamental bases of the Constitution, nor to change the distribution of public powers.

It is composed of the current representatives of the Legislature as increased by the doubling of the territorial representation.

Thus it will reach a total of nine hundred and ninety members.

Section Three

Of the Constituent Body

The Constituent Body is the Assembly of representatives possessed of the right of revising the Constitution in its entirety, of changing the distribution of the public powers, and of creating a new Constitution.

It is composed of the current representatives of the legislature as increased by the doubling of the representation on the basis of population and taxable capacity.

Thus it will reach a total of nine hundred and ninety members.

Section Four

Of the Demand for a National Convention or Constituent Body, and of the Nomination of Additional Representatives

Citizens may address, in their own names, individual petitions to the legislature, and demand the convocation of a National Convention or Constituent Body.

But the legislature alone may decide, in the name of the Nation, whether it thinks such a convocation necessary.

It makes this declaration by a public act, which is not submitted for the sanction of the King.

When it is a question of a National Convention, this act must contain a precise statement of the articles of the constitution, which the legislature believes to require examination, or of the object of the addition which it judges to be necessary.

When it is a question of the Constituent Body, this act must state only the explicit desire for the convocation of this body.

The legislature can in no case add to this exposition details of its motives, nor indicate the nature of the reform or change.

The members of the legislature which has proclaimed this act cannot be elected members of the following legislature.

The following legislature will cause this act to be deliberated upon in the month in which the second session opens.

If it rejects the proposition, it will decree this in these terms: The National Legislative Assembly decrees that there is no occasion to form a National Convention, or that there is no occasion to assemble the Constituent Body.

Then the proposition shall be regarded as though it had never been made.

If the legislature admits the proposition, it will declare this in these terms: The National Legislative Assembly decrees that there is occasion to form a National Convention, or that there is occasion to assemble the Constituent Body.

In this case the members of this second legislature cannot be elected members of the following legislature.

The legislature which immediately succeeds will be compelled to deliberate in the month in which its first session opens, and before passing to other acts on the same proposition.

If it rejects it, it will decree this in these terms: The National Legislative Assembly decrees that there is no occasion to form a National Convention, or that there is no occasion to assemble the Constituent Body.

Then the proposition will be regarded as though it had never been made.

If the legislature approves the proposition, it will decree it in these terms: The National Legislative Assembly decrees that the National Convention will be formed, or that the Constituent Body will be assembled without delay, to take into consideration the objects indicated in the act of . . . day, proclaimed by the National Legislative Assembly of . . . year.

By virtue of this decree the electors will be convoked in each department, at the beginning of the month of June, in accordance with the forms prescribed by the Constitution.

They will assemble in the usual place of election on the 19th of the same month.

If it is a matter of forming a National Convention, they will nominate in each department the number of representatives attributed to its territory.

If it is a matter of forming a Constituent Body, they will nominate the same number of representatives which will have been sent to the last legislature, by reason of the population and direct contribution of the department.

Section Five
Of the Assembly of Representatives in the National Convention

The new representatives, nominated in each department to form the Convention, will unite with the legislature in its meeting place on the 8th day of June.

The president of the legislature will leave the chair, and the united representatives will assemble provisionally under the presidency of the oldest member, to verify the powers of the additional representatives alone.

On the 14th July, whatever may be the number of members present, they will constitute themselves as a National Convention.

The representatives will pronounce together, in the name of the French people, the oath *to live freely or die.*

They will then take individually the oath 'to maintain with all their power the fundamental bases of the Constitution of the Kingdom, decreed by the Constituent Assembly during the years 1789, 1790 and 1791; to make no attack upon the distribution of public powers; and to limit themselves to making enactments on the objects enumerated in the act proclaimed by the legislative assembly of the . . . year'.

The National Convention will take up its duties from this moment.

It will not be called a Convention except in so far as acts relative to the objects of its Assembly are concerned. They will receive the pure and simple assent of the King.

But all acts of pure legislation which it may make during the duration of its exercise are submitted for the sanction.

The National Convention cannot prolong itself beyond the term designated for the return of the legislature.

But it may dissolve itself before this date, as soon as it has fulfilled the object of its mission.

In this case, the additional representatives will retire, and the legislative body will resume the same form which it had on the day of assembly.

Section Six and Last
Of the Assembly of Representatives in a Constituent Body

The representatives, nominated in each department to form the Constituent Body, will unite with the legislative body in the place of its meeting on the 8th July.

The verification of the powers of the additional representatives will be performed in the manner indicated in the preceding section.

On the 14th July, whatever may be the number of members present, they will declare themselves the National Constituent Assembly.

The National Constituent Assembly of the years 1789, 1790 and 1791 declares that this is the limit of its capacity and the end of its powers; the Constituent Body cannot receive any rules except from itself; it has nothing to prescribe to it; it will find all in this motto, which it thus transmits: *Equality: live freely or die.*

BIBLIOGRAPHY

THE DEBATES

Les Archives Parlementaires, Vols. VIII, IX, XXV, XXVI, XXIX, XXX.
Le Moniteur Universel, 1789–91, Vols. I to V.
Histoire Parlementaire de la Révolution Française (Buchez et Roux), Vols. I to XV.
Choix de Rapports, Opinions et Discours (Paris, 1819), Vols. I to VIII.

GENERAL WORKS

AULARD, A.: *Histoire Politique de la Révolution Française* (Paris, 1920).
DESLANDRES, M.: *Histoire Constitutionnelle de la France*, Vol. I (Paris, 1938).
ESMEIN, A., and NEZARD, H.: *Elements de Droit Constitutionnel Français et Comparé* (2 vols.), 8th edition (Paris, 1928).
JANET, P.: *Histoire de la Science Politique* (2 vols.), 5th edition (Paris, 1924).
LANSON, G.: *Histoire de la Littérature Française*, 8th edition (Paris, 1903).
LEFEBVRE, G., GUYOT, R., and SAGNAC, P.: *La Révolution Française* (Paris, 1930).
SÉE, H.: *Science et Philosophie de l'Histoire* (Paris, 1928).
TAINE, H.: *Les Origines de la France Contemporaine*
    (i) *L'Ancien Régime*
    (ii) *La Révolution*, Vol. I (Paris, 1894).
VILLAT, L.: *La Révolution et l'Empire*, Vol. I (Paris, 1936).

CONTEMPORARY AUTHORS

BAILLY, J. S.: *Mémoires d'un Témoin de la Révolution* (3 vols.), (Paris, 1804).
BARÈRE, B.: *Mémoires* (trans. Payen-Payne) (London, 1896).
BERGASSE, N.: *Discours sur le Pouvoir Législatif et le Pouvoir Exécutif dans une Monarchie* (Paris, 1789).
BUZOT, F. H. L.: *Mémoires sur la Révolution Française* (Paris, 1823).
LAFAYETTE, MARQUIS DE: *Mémoires à l'Histoire de l'Assemblée Constituante* (2 vols.) (Paris, 1824).
MOUNIER, J. J.: *Recherches sur les Causes qui ont empêché les Français de devenir Libres* (3 vols.) (Paris, 1822).
RABAUT DE ST. ETIENNE: *Historiques Pièces de la Révolution Française* (3 vols.) (Paris, 1801).
ROEDERER, P. C.: *Esprit de la Révolution* (Paris, 1831).
SIEYÈS, E. J.: *Qu'est ce que le Tiers-Etat?* (Paris, 1789).

SPECIAL WORKS, MONOGRAPHS, MEMOIRS, ETC.

ADAMS, R. G.: *Political Ideas of the American Revolution* (New York, 1939).
ALENGRY, F.: *La Déclaration des Droits de l'Homme et du Citoyen* (Pamphlet, Paris 1901).
AULARD, A.: *Les Orateurs de la Révolution: l'Assemblée Constituante* (Paris, 1905).
BASTID, P.: *Sieyès et sa Pensée* (Paris, 1939).
BOISSENOT, P. E.: *Les Opinions Politiques de Barnave* (Paris, 1919).
BONNO, G.: *La Constitution Britannique devant l'Opinion Française de Montesquieu à Bonaparte* (Paris, 1913).
BOUCHARD, A.: *Le Club Breton* (Paris, 1920).
BOUGEART, A.: *Danton. Documents Authentiques pour servir à l'Histoire de la Révolution Française* (Paris, 1861).

CARCASSONNE, E.: *Montesquieu et la Problème de la Constitution Française au XVIIIe siècle* (Paris, 1927).

CARRÉ, H.: *La Noblesse de France et l'Opinion Publique au XVIIIe siècle* (Paris, 1920).

—— *La Fin des Parlements* (Paris, 1912).

CAUDEL, M.: *Nos Libertés Politiques* (Paris, 1910).

CHAMPION, E.: *Rousseau et la Révolution Française* (Paris, 1909).

—— *La France d'après les Cahiers de 1789* (Paris, 1897).

COCHIN, A.: *Les Sociétés de Pensée et la Democratie* (Paris, 1921).

—— *Les Sociétés de Pensée et la Révolution en Bretagne* (2 vols.), (Paris, 1925).

DELAGRANGE, R.: *Le Premier Comité de la Constitution de la Constituante* (Paris, 1900).

DUCLOS, P.: *La Notion de Constitution dans l'Œuvre de l'Assemblée Constituante de 1789* (Paris, 1932).

DUGUIT, L.: *La Séparation des Pouvoirs et l'Assemblée Nationale de 1789* (Paris, 1893).

FABRE, J. *Les Pères de la Révolution* (Paris, 1910).

FAGUET, E.: *Dix-Huitième Siècle—Etudes Littéraires* (Paris, 1902).

—— *Politique Comparée de Montesquieu, Rousseau et Voltaire* (Paris, 1902).

FAŸ, B.: *L'Esprit Révolutionnaire en France et aux Etats-Unis à la fin du XVIIIe siècle* (Paris, 1924).

FONTENEAU, M.: *Du Pouvoir Constituante en France* (Caen, 1900).

FUSIL, C. A.: *L'Anti-Rousseau* (Paris, 1929).

GAUTHEROT, G.: *L'Assemblée Constituante* (Paris, 1914).

GAZIER, A.: *Etudes sur L'Histoire Religieuse de la Révolution* (Paris, 1887).

GIRAUD, E.: *L'Œuvre d'Organisation Judiciaire de L'Assemblée Nationale Constituante* (Paris, 1921).

HERRIOT, E.: *Aux Sources de la Liberté* (Paris, 1939).

JELLINEK, G.: *La Déclaration des Droits de l'Homme et du Citoyen* (Paris, 1902).

LECOCQ, A.: *La Question Sociale au XVIIIe siècle* (Paris, 1909).

LICHTENBERGER, A.: *Le Socialisme et la Révolution Française* (Paris, 1899).

MAISTRE, JOSEPH DE: *Considérations sur la France* (ed. Chernovitz, Paris, 1910).

MARCAGGI, V.: *Les Origines de la Déclaration des Droits de l'Homme de 1789* (Paris, 1912).

MARTIN, K.: *French Liberal Thought in the Eighteenth Century* (London, 1929).

MATHIEZ, A.: *Etudes Robespierristes* (especially Chaps. 7, 8) (Paris, 1917).

—— *Girondins et Montagnards* (Paris, 1930).

—— *La Révolution et L'Eglise* (Paris, 1910).

—— *Le Club des Cordeliers* (Paris, 1910).

—— *Rome et le Clergé Français sous la Constituante* (Paris, 1911).

MELLIS, PAUL DE: *Le Principe de la Séparation des Pouvoirs* (Toulouse, 1907).

MORNET, D.: *Les Origines Intellectuelles de la Révolution Française.* 3rd edition (Paris, 1936).

—— *La Pensée Française au XVIIIe siècle* (Paris, 1932).

ROUSTAN, M.: *Pioneers of the French Revolution* (trans. Frederic Whyte, London, 1926).

SÉE, HENRI: *La Vie Economique et les Classes Sociales en France au XVIIIe siècle* (Paris, 1924).

VIALAY, A.: *Les Cahiers de Doléances du Tiers-Etat* (Paris, 1911).

WALCH, P.: *La Déclaration des Droits de l'Homme et du Citoyen, et l'Assemblée Constituante* (Paris, 1903).

WRIGHT, E. H.: *The Meaning of Rousseau* (London, 1929).

INDEX